Hiding In Plain Sight

The Pee Dee Indians after Contact

.By Claude W. Chavis, Jr.

Cover Art: Girls on a Pony. By David Locklear.

Photographs by the author and Gene J. Crediford.

Library of Congress Cataloging – in – Publication Data

Chavis, Claude W., Jr.

Hiding In Plain Sight: The Pee Dee Indians after Contact/Claude W. Chavis, Jr.

Includes bibliographical references and works cited.

ISBNISBN-13: 978-0615458250 (PDIN Press)

ISBN-10: 0615458254

1. Native American. 2. History. 3. Pee Dee. 4. Indian. 5. Carolina.

Published in the United States of America.

Dedicated to my daughters, Crystal and Sarah.

Love, Dad.

Foreword

In the fall 2004, I began meeting with UNCP colleagues Michael Spivey and Ottis Murray concerning the vision of an annual Southeast Indian Studies Conference; it was an initiative independent of the American Indian Studies department that we planned, however, with their support. Both Michael, who had focused his dissertation upon the Pee Dee Indians, and Ottis, a sociologist, were extremely interested in the survival of local Indians and the issues they faced; we saw the conference as a way of bringing the somewhat disparate communities – Indians, scholars, and non-Indians – together with a chance to explore and communicate both the historical and contemporary problems faced by Indians in the southeast. It was intended to be a conference that brought scholars and laymen alike together within a forum so as to articulate, communicate and explore the problems and potential solutions in southeast Indian country. In noting this endeavor, I am deliberate in supplying a means to acknowledge Claude Chavis who attended the first conference freely sharing his insights with the community so gathered.

Claude was a prominent figure at the initial conference; he sat attentively in the front row taking in all the presentations and discussions. As such, he quickly came to my notice and we were soon engaging in meaningful discussion spilling forth from and beyond the conference. It was clear to me that he was and is a man of intellectual substance with much to contribute to informing Indian history in the Southeast. When the conference came to a close, I was pleased with the prospect of working with this new friend and scholar in Indian country.

In the coming year, much to my surprise and delight, Claude appeared at the university; he signed into several of my classes and it was simply a pleasure to have someone so knowledgeable in my classroom; with his preparations and accomplishments, it was a pleasure to engage him in discussions and have his insights shared with the other students. As a professor of long standing accomplishment, I was delighted with the manner in which he improved his fellow students and shared his storied insights with them; it was a teacher's dream to have such a student. As Claude completed a concentration in American Indian Studies, he shined brightly and it was clear that his passion for the subject was more than a vocation.

Afterwards Claude began a graduate program in Social Studies education as a means to further his Indian studies and career interests; as he researched Pee Dee history, it was clear to me that he would make a great contribution to the acknowledgement of surviving Natives in the Southeast. As a Tribal Historian, Claude had long explored the questions of Indian survival in the Carolinas. Despite my efforts to suggest topical concerns and interests, he knew the critical questions to ask and answer in his research.

During my study of Native survivals in Virginia and the Carolinas, I had begun to outline the historic apartheid conditions fostered upon American Indians in the south. In this regard, there was a long standing practice designed to transfer Native Americans into the segregated colored category; hence many Indians simply disappeared from public records in paper genocide. Notwithstanding the indigenous peoples remained only to suffer the limitations of freedom imposed upon them and their identity. It is this story of apartheid applied to Native Americans in the south that Claude and other scholars have had to confront as a means of restoring the identity and dignity of being Indian in the south.

Acknowledging these factors of apartheid existence and Indian survival, Claude introduces his readers to the simple fact of Indian survival in plain sight despite the best colonial efforts to extinguish their presence in the Pee Dee river basin. Providing an origin legend, Claude summarizes a "prehistory" that may date fifty thousand years before the arrival of Europeans in the Americas.

In this work of Pee Dee affirmation, Claude's approach established within the standards of contemporary historical scholarship; he tracks the historical events from encounter through colonialism and segregation into contemporary times. Through the process a picture emerges of an indigenous people – the Pee Dee – who never left the region and maintained their Native identity through all challenges. The Pee Dee surface as a vibrant people who assisted the revolutionaries to establish the United States only to lose much of their freedoms to apartheid centered state and local governments that were bound and determined to erase the indigenous population from the official records. Although the Pee Dee were not included in the Indian removals, their fate was shackled to the segregation policies of the state and region. Despite these oppressive policies and their application upon aboriginal peoples, the Pee Dee Natives like others in the southeast managed to survive and even thrive in making their way into the twenty-first century. It is their story with its triumph of aboriginal will that Claude gives us in this historical documentation of the Pee Dee tribe emergent in today's map of Indian country.

Jay Hansford C. Vest, Ph.D.
Enrolled member Monacan Indian Nation
Direct descendent Opechcanough (Pamunkey)
Honorary Pikuni (Blackfeet) in ceremonial adoption (June 1989)
Professor, Department of American Indian Studies
University of North Carolina at Pembroke
One University Drive (P. O. Box 1510)
Pembroke, NC 28372-1510

Table of Contents

Foreword vii

Acknowledgements xi

Prologue 1

Chapter 1: The Pee Dee and Creation 5

Chapter 2: The Pee Dee Encounter Europeans 14

Chapter 3: They Called Them The Snake People 18

Chapter 4: The Pee Dee and the Colonial Period 24

Chapter 5: Pee Dee References in Colonial Records 32

Chapter 6: Pee Dee Participation in the American Revolution 50

Chapter 7: The Aftermath of the Fight for Freedom 58

Chapter 8: The Pee Dee and Share Cropping 64

Chapter 9: The Churches and the Pee Dee 70

Chapter 10: Pee Dee and the Schools 76

Chapter 11: The Pee Dee Emerge from the Shadows 80

Epilogue 86

Appendix A: The Town Creek Ceremonial Center 88

Appendix B: South Carolina Slave Code 92

Appendix C: Burnt Swamp Baptist Association 98

Endnotes 100

Acknowledgements

Writing this story was in many ways a cooperative exercise. I am grateful to the professors of the University of North Carolina at Pembroke for their guidance and patience over the past 5 years. Dr. Scott Billingsley, Dr. Jeffrey Fredericks, Dr. Michael Spivey, and Dr. Rosemarie Stremlau showed me a more analytical way of looking at history and encouraged me to pursue my research. I am especially grateful to Dr. Jay H. Vest for his guidance along the Red Road.

I must also acknowledge the assistance of the Smithsonian Institute whose gracious grant enabled me to pursue my research in our nation's capital among its abundant resources and provided endless steams of information and photographs. My doctoral program mentor, Dr. Timothy Green, of Walden University, also played a significant part in the final development of this book.

Finally I must thank my family and tribe for their help and support in recording this history. Of course, any and all mistakes are my responsibility and do not reflect on anyone else.

Prologue

What follows is the story of the Pee Dee Indians from their prehistoric arrival in the Americas to the present. This is a story tied to the Pee Dee River and the land surrounding it. This is a story of a people who for decades were invisible to mainstream Americans. This is a story of adaptation, assimilation, resistance, and resurgence; this is the story of our ancestors.

This narrative provides the background, evidence, and references to substantiate the first three criteria of the Federal Recognition process. According to the 2000 U.S. census, nearly 14,000 American Indians and Alaska natives lived in South Carolina. If we add to this number the over 27,000 mixed race people who declared Native American ancestry, we arrive at a total of approximately 41,000 South Carolinians who identified as Indian.[1] In 1790, only about 300 Indian people lived in the Piedmont and low country.

How did they survive and thrive, not merely as individuals who can point to an Indian in the family tree, but as communities of people who lay claim to an Indian identity? Three strategies for survival – resistance to racial reclassification, tribal land holding, and assimilation – provide an answer.[2]

Let us start with the name Pee Dee. According to Frank G. Speck, "While neither river nor tribes are known to the present Catawba, the name may be turned into a meaning in their dialect. By manipulation Pee Dee comes to sound like pi^ri, 'something good', or pi^hare, 'smart*, 'expert', 'capable', whence ye pi-'hare, 'people clever'." (Pronounced Peri, Pe-h're)[3]

An alternate explanation for the name Pee Dee involves the Spanish. When Juan Pardo's second expedition to South Carolina visited the Chiefdom of Cofitachequi in the late 1560's, his notary, Juan de la Bandera, recorded the existence of a tribe on the Pee Dee River called Vehidi (Ve-ee-dee) in their language.[4] This may have been corrupted over the years into Pee Dee. The tribe has lived for at least a thousand years along the river which is also called the Pee Dee.

According to Joseph Epes Brown, the primal foundations of Native American traditions include:

- Religion is inseparable from daily life

- Words have a special potency or force

- Telling a story recreates the place and events

- Arts and handicrafts carry Power[5]

- Time is cyclical and reciprocal

- An intense quality relationship with nature is most important[6]

These primal foundations of Native American traditions tie them to the land of their ancestors. Each member of the Pee Dee seeks whenever possible to remain at home, close to their ancestors and their roots. For the Pee Dee, place is important, and religious practices are often localized. Participation is more important than belief.

Cooperation with and devotion to the larger kin group is a central part of small-scale societies, and this is true of Native American communities. Teaching proper behavior toward others, which is defined by one's relationship to them, is an essential part of child rearing. The core value is the expectation that the entire world, one's life, and one's other-than-human relatives will be treated in the same way as all human relatives. Included in those values is an enduring sense of the importance of place.[7] All of these factors tied the Pee Dee to their homeland. They have resisted innumerable attempts to displace them. Brown suggests that European racial attitudes have devalued other cultural traditions and that these people generally have been relegated to positions of inferior status in the larger (domain) society. Denied the possibility of social or cultural mobility, many of these groups seek cohesion and identity within their own communities.[8]

The Pee Dee have survived by **<u>hiding in plain sight</u>** in the Pee Dee River basin, our original home land. By passing in the outside world as Black, mulatto, or even White for centuries, our ancestors maintained the "secret" of their identities. In doing so, much of our heritage and traditions have been lost and are only now being restored.

Chapter 1: The Pee Dee and Creation

In Pee Dee tradition, knowledge is passed on orally, through stories. Each story has a lesson or moral embedded in it. Let us begin our history with the story of the creation of this world.

There was a world before this world, but the Great Mysterious, the Great Creator, was not pleased with that world. He said to himself: "I will make a new world." Reaching into his pipe bag, he took out his pipe and sacred tobacco, placing them on top of the bag. He sang three songs, bringing a heavy rain. When he sang the first song, it started to rain. When he sang the second, it poured. When he sang the third, the rain-swollen rivers overflowed their banks. But when he sang a fourth song and stamped on the Earth, it split open in many places like a shattered gourd, and water flowed from the cracks until it covered everything. The Great Mysterious floated on his huge pipe bag. He let himself be carried by waves and wind this way and that, drifting for a long time.

After a long time, the rain stopped, and everything had drowned. Only the crow survived, though it had no place to rest and was very tired. Flying above the Great Mysterious, three times, Crow asked him to make a place for it to land and rest.

The Great Mysterious thought: "It's time to open the pipe bag and unwrap my pipe."

The wrapping and the pipe bag contained all manner of animals and birds, from which he selected four animals known for their ability to swim under water for a long time. First he sang a song and took the loon out of the bag. He commanded the loon to dive and bring up a lump of mud. The loon did dive, but it brought up nothing.

The Great Mysterious sang a second song and took the otter out of the bag. He ordered the otter to dive and bring up some mud. The sleek otter at once dived into the water, using its strong webbed feet to go down, down, down. It was submerged for a long time, but when it finally came to the surface, it brought nothing.

Taking the beaver out of the pipe's wrapping, the Great Mysterious sang a third song. He commanded the beaver to go deep beneath the water and bring some mud. The beaver thrust itself into the water, using its great tail to propel itself downward. It stayed under water longer than the others, but when it finally came up again, it too brought nothing.

At last the Great Mysterious sang the fourth song and took the turtle out of the bag. The turtle is very strong. Among our people it stands for long life and endurance and the power to survive. A turtle heart is great medicine, for it keeps on beating a long time after the turtle is dead.

"You must bring up mud," the Great Mysterious told the turtle. It dove into the water and stayed below so long that the other three animals shouted: "The turtle is dead; it will never come up again!"

All the time, the crow was flying around and begging for a place to light. After what seemed to be eons, the turtle broke the surface of the water and paddled to the Great Mysterious. "I got to the bottom!" the turtle cried. "I found some mud!" And sure enough, its feet and claws, even the space in the cracks on its sides between its upper and lower shell,were filled with mud.

Scooping mud from the turtle's feet and sides, the Great Mysterious began to sing. He sang all the while that he shaped the mud in his hands and spread it on the water to make a spot of dry land for him. When he had sung the fourth song, there was enough land for the Great Mysterious and for the crow.

"Come down and rest," said the Great Mysterious to the crow, and the bird was glad to. Then the Great Mysterious took from his bag two long wing feathers of the eagle. He waved them over his plot of ground and commanded it to spread until it covered everything. Soon all the water was replaced by earth.

"Water without land is not good," thought the Great Mysterious, "but land without water is not good either." Feeling Pity for the land, he wept for the Earth and the creatures he would put upon it, and his tears were the rain that became the oceans, streams, and lakes. "That's better," he thought.

Out of his pipe bag the Great Mysterious took all kinds of animals, birds, plants and scattered them over the land. When he stamped on the earth, they all came alive. From the earth the Great Mysterious formed the shapes of men and women. He used Red earth and White earth, Black earth and Yellow earth, and made as many as he thought would do for a start. He stamped on the earth and the shapes came alive, each taking the color of the earth out of which it was made. The Great Mysterious gave all of them understanding and speech and told them what tribes they belonged to. The Great Mysterious said to them:

"The first world I made was bad; the creatures on it were bad. So I burned it up. The second world I made was also bad, so I drowned it. This is the third world I have made." The Great Mysterious continued: "Now, if you learn to behave like human beings and live in peace with each other and with the other living things, the two-legged, the four-legged, the many-legged, the fliers, the no-legs, the green plants of this universe, then all will be well. But if you do not, then I will destroy this world too. The future depends on you."

The Great Mysterious gave the people the pipe. "Live by it," he said. He named this land the Turtle Continent in honor of the turtle who came up with the mud of which the third world was made.

"Someday there might be a fourth world," the Great Mysterious thought. Then he rested.[9]

The legend of the Creation of this world may or may not be true, but modern science does not support the story. Scientific evidenced tells a different story; according to science, the story of the Pee Dee does not begin on another world but on the far side of this world in Siberia. Most archeologists believe that the first people migrated to America across a land bridge between Siberia and Alaska during the last Ice Age.

However, recent archaeological finds and geophysical studies have dramatically challenged this picture, advancing the possibility that people traveled both by boat and by foot.[10] The ancestors of the American Indians or Native Americans may have arrived more than 50,000 years ago. They spread throughout the Americas in the centuries that followed, finally reaching North and South Carolina. Recent archeological discoveries in Topper, South Carolina have found evidence of human occupation there approximately 50,000 years ago.[11]

During that time, Native American cultures developed, flourished, and changed. Their technologies evolved, as shown by the varieties of artifacts such as arrowheads and pottery they left behind for us to find.

There were major four periods in the Prehistory of South Carolina and the Americas as a whole: Paleo-Indian, Archaic, Woodland, and Mississippian. Each of these periods reflected a distinct culture or way of life.

Overlapping the Woodland Period, the Mississippian Period, from 900 A.D. to 1750 A.D., was much like the Woodland, but included larger villages associated with temple mounds. Mississippian groups appear to have been limited to the southern and western portions of our state. Both the Woodland and Mississippian Periods often built stockades or palisades around their villages. The tools of the Mississippian villagers were similar to the more prevalent Woodland people, with the addition of new ceramic designs and art motifs, as well as the construction of elaborate temple mounds and political centers. Between 900 A.D. and the 1600s, South Carolina's Pee Dee societies were in transition from the Woodland to Mississippian.

Just because tribes followed a Woodland or Mississippian life style did not mean they were all identical. Individual tribal customs and beliefs varied greatly. Tribes also differed ethnically and linguistically. In fact, there were three major languages in South Carolina: Iroquoian, Siouan, and Algonquian.

Little is known about the early Pee Dee. However, we do know that they manufactured clay pottery, occupied their settlements for several months each year, but not year round, and planted gardens. Using digging sticks or stone (and sometimes shell) hoes, they raised marsh elder, squash, bottle gourds, sunflower, May grass, and goosefoot from small gardens. These native plants give strong evidence that farming evolved independently in the area. After 200 A.D. seed corn appeared, apparently traded from tribes in the Southwest.[12]

Most scientists now agree that Zea may (maize) was developed from two Mexican grasses known as Zea tripsacum (tripsacum) and Zea mexicana (teosinte). Evidence points to the ancient Mayans near the Isthmus of Tehuantepec. Archeologists have found evidence of the spread of maize from there throughout the Americans long before the first Europeans arrived.

Using simple tools, the Pee Dee cleared garden plots in the forests that covered the Carolinas and planted their crops. The Native American name for corn means "our life" or "it sustains us."

The cultivation of corn draws heavily on the nutrients in the soil and requires intensive labor. This meant that the tribe had the use extremely rich soils, such as bottomlands along the Pee Dee River, and had to labor long and hard in preparing the fields, hoeing weeds, and keeping birds and animals away from the corn. This required a more structured society to better organize and control the needed workers. As a result, the Pee Dee developed more centralized government and social structures. Societies' emphasis was placed on the chiefs; they and their immediate kin were considered descendants of the sun, making them divine. Large earthen mounds were constructed as a way of separating the chief and his family from the rest of the tribe.

The resulting chiefdoms had the military might to overwhelm smaller tribes; this led to a rapid spread of Mississippian culture throughout the southeast. Some archeologists and historians theorize that each chiefdom rule a single river basin system such as the Pee Dee. By 1200, the Pee Dee had built a ceremonial center at Town Creek surrounded by a palisade.

Pee Dee tribal Elders tell us the evil spirits must travel in a straight line. Therefore, a circular palisade with a curved entrance was appropriate for a burial mound. This provided for the well-being of the souls resting there.

Hunting game and gathering wild plants remained very important, even with the advent of farming. Most food comes from acorns, hickory nuts and a variety of other nuts, fruits, and wild vegetables. White-tailed deer were the primary source of meat, but bear, turkey, raccoon, fish, and waterfowl were also important. Fish and shellfish were very important foods for tribes on the Coastal Plain.

Native American and Pee Dee cultures are the "cornerstone" of Southern cuisine. From their cultures came one of the main staples of the Southern diet: corn (maize), either ground into meal or limed with an alkaline salt to make hominy, also called masa, in a process known as nixtamalization.[14] Corn has been used to make all kinds of dishes from the familiar cornbread and grits to liquors such as whiskey and moonshine, which were important trade items.

Though a lesser staple, potatoes were also Native American and were used in many similar ways as corn. Native Americans also used many other vegetables still familiar on southern tables. Squash, pumpkin, many types of beans, tomatoes, many types of peppers and sassafras all came to the settlers via the native tribes.

Many fruits are available in this region. Muscadines, Blackberries, raspberries, and many other wild berries were part of Pee Dees' diet.

"To a far greater degree than anyone realizes several of the most important food dishes of the Southeastern Indians live on today in the "soul food" eaten by both Black and White Southerners. Hominy, for example, is still eaten ... Sofkee live on as grits ... cornbread [is] used by Southern cooks ... Indian fritters ... variously known as "hoe cake," ... or "Johnny cake."... Indians boiled cornbread is present in Southern cuisine as "corn meal dumplings," ... and as "hush puppies," ... Southerners cook their beans and field peas by boiling them, as did the Indians ... like the Indians they cure their meat and smoke it over hickory." [15]

Pee Dees also supplemented their diets with meats derived from the hunting of native game. Venison was an important meat staple due to the abundance of White-tailed deer in the area. They also hunted rabbits, squirrels, opossums, and raccoons. Later livestock, adopted from Europeans, in the form of hogs and cattle were kept. When game or livestock was killed, the entire animal was used. Aside from the meat, it was not uncommon for them to eat organ meats such as liver, brains and intestines.

This tradition remains today in hallmark dishes like chitterlings (commonly called chit'lins) which are fried large intestines of hogs, livermush (a common dish in the Carolinas made from hog liver), and pork brains and eggs. The fat of the animals, particularly hogs, was rendered and used for cooking and frying. Many of the early settlers were taught Pee Dee cooking methods.

House shapes varied from region to region, some people built rectangular homes, while others lived in round houses. They built houses by putting saplings side-by-side and upright in the ground. Sticks were woven between them and covered with bark, thatch, or mud. Roofs were made in one of two ways. The saplings forming the wall were pulled together at the top and tied, or other saplings are placed horizontally over the outside walls and supported on posts placed in the center of the house. A clay-lined hole hardened from heat was left in the roof for smoke from a centrally placed fire to escape.

Several pottery styles occurred during the early Woodland. Potters used crushed steatite, quartz, or sand for temper to help keep the vessels from breaking during firing. Most pots had tapered bottoms, which let the vessel sit upright in the deep ash of cooking hearths. They decorated their pottery by stamping the surfaces with either cord or textile-wrapped or carved wooden paddles before firing.

Because the stone projectile points changed shape and size during the Woodland period, archeologists know that the bow and arrow replaced the spear and atlatl. Typically, Woodland people placed few offerings in graves. When they did, they were useful or personal items, such as stone arrow tips, chisels, smoking pipes, clay pots, or jewelry.

Chapter 2: The Pee Dee Encounter Europeans

Before Sir Walter Raleigh's expedition landed on the Outer Banks in 1585, French and Spanish explorers traveled across modern-day South Carolina claiming American land. By 1520s, the Spanish, in particular, were winning the race of conquest. Early Spanish explorers included Luis Vasquez de Allyan, who sailed the Cape Fear River in 1526; Hernando de Soto, who in 1540 traversed through the southern Appalachian mountains; and Juan Pardo, who led two expeditions from Santa Elena (Parris Island, South Carolina) into the Catawba Valley and then into the mountains of western North Carolina and Eastern Tennessee.

During his first expedition, Pardo established good relationships with Indian tribes and searched primarily for food for the Santa Elena settlement. The second expedition's mission was mainly to find a road to Zacatecas, Mexico (location of Spanish silver mines) and to claim land for Spain.[16]

The first expedition lasted from December 1, 1566 to March 7, 1567. Pardo and 125 men traveled northward from Santa Elena to find Indian towns with food. After traveling through the swampland of northeastern South Carolina, Pardo stopped at Yssa and then later at Jaora, an Indian town near modern-day Morganton. There, the Spanish explorer and his men constructed Fort San Juan. Pardo and his remaining men (Sergeant Hernando Moyano de Morales and thirty men garrisoned the fort) followed the Catawba River and visited the towns of Quinahaqui (near Catawba) and Guatari (near Salisbury).

Along the way, Pardo met with caciques (Spanish term for tribal leader) and through an interpreter informed Indians that they were Spanish subjects. Pardo also left behind his chaplain and a few soldiers to evangelize the Indians. According to anthropologist/historian Charles Hudson and as evidenced by the second expedition, Pardo must have also instructed Indians to build houses for the Spanish troops and to store corn exclusively for Spanish troops.

Meanwhile, Sergeant Moyano and his men at Fort San Juan searched for minerals and helped a rival tribe defeat the Chiscas. While Pardo explored, General Pedro Menendez de Aviles feared a French attack and ordered Pardo, unaware of Moyano's actions, back to Santa Elena. He returned on March 7, 1567.[17]

Impressed with Pardo's good reports, Menendez ordered a second expedition. On September 1, 1567, Pardo started leading approximately 90 to 120 men back into the Catawba Valley and the mountains of North Carolina--and this time into Tennessee--in search of a road to Zacatecas. During the journey, they were fed by Indians who had stored corn exclusively for Spaniards. Before returning to Jaora, Pardo met with Guatari Mico and Orata Chiquini—two female caciques. After a short stay in the town, Pardo headed for the mountains to assist Moyano. The Spaniard found Moyano and his men penned in a fort but unhurt.

Later Pardo avoided a surprise attack and decided to return to Santa Elena. On the return, Pardo and his men built two more forts. The second expedition ended on March 2, 1568, at Santa Elena. Pardo did not help settle LaFlorida for Spain, for the forts were too far inland and the forts were eventually abandoned.[18]

When Juan Pardo's second expedition to South Carolina visited the Chiefdom of Cofitachequi in the late 1560's, his notary, Juan de la Bandera, recorded the existence of a tribe on the Pee Dee River called Vehidi (Ve-ee-dee) in their language.[19] Pardo went out of his way to visit Ylasi, where he meet chiefs Uca Orata, Tagaya Orata, and Sarutti Orata. Clearly Ylasi was a town of some importance within Cofitachequi. It is probable that Ylasi controlled the Pee Dee River.[20]

The Vehidi (Pee Dee) Indians lived in all along the Pee Dee River, from the areas around Town Creek in North Carolina to the mouth of the river at Winyah Bay.[21] They were an agriculturally-based tribe, and cultivated crops such as squash, marsh elder, chenopodium, sumpweed, may grass, knotweed and sunflower.[22] They lived .in small villages along the river. Populations were necessarily small because of the difficulty in supporting large numbers of people with this manner of subsistence.

The homes for the tribe ranged from townhouses similar to those of the Cherokee to dome-shaped wattle arid daub structures made by hardening clay on top of a skeleton of wooden posts.[23] These Woodland-era people were already developing a tradition of building earthen mounds, which often served primarily for burials but occasionally were in the shape of animals or geometric shapes. [24]

The society practiced gender equality. While the chief of the tribe was an inherited position, he was viewed as a servant of his people. Often, he assumed the name of the tribe. European explorers mistakenly believed this meant he was without equal, but it was really a sign that he was one of the people. While duties were divided along gender lines, with men hunting and fishing while the women tended the fields and made pottery, these roles were by no means rigid and neither role was considered superior to the other. Tribal Council had both male and female members; there were both male and female war captains; and matrilineal kinship was the norm in the Southeast with lineage traced through the mother.

This gender equality became one of the victims of European contact. In order to show their greatness, chiefs had to be capable of giving away a great deal. Pardo, in his gift giving to the Indians, perhaps understood this. But, Pardo offered gifts only to the male chiefs of the tribes and the male sons or nephews of the female chiefs of the tribes. Some of those gifts have been found at southeastern archaeological sites.[25]

European culture did not generally accept women in positions of authority. European men conducted the commerce of the day and often refused to negotiate with the "weaker sex." Later as the trade in deerskins became an important part of relationships, American Indian women were relegated to the positions of "squaws". Squaw is the phonetic spelling of an eastern Algonquian Indian word, meaning "woman." It has been used as a noun or adjective, its present meaning is an indigenous woman of North America, regardless of tribe. The term has been considered offensive, especially since the late 20th Century.[26]

The Pee Dee spoke a Siouan-based language similar in many ways to those of the tribes living near them and while they were a dominant force in the area, they lived a reasonably peaceful existence with the tribes which surrounded them. The following chart places the Pee Dee (Pedee) language in the Pedee branch of the Catawba division of the Siouan stock. For the most part the Pee Dee have lost their language and speak American English almost exclusively. Some effort has been made to reintroduce the language to the younger generations.

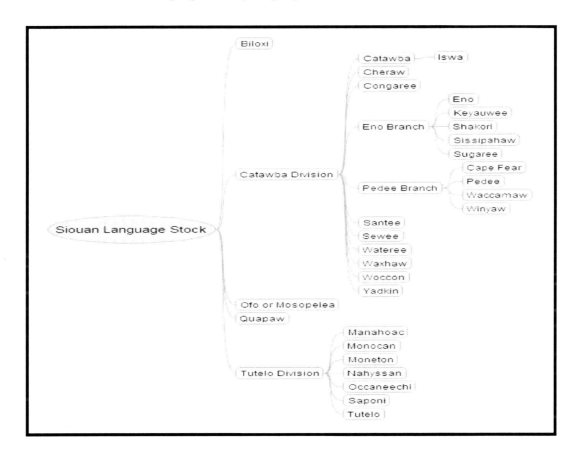

Chapter 3: They Called Them The Snake People

The Spanish explorers met the Pee Dee Indians of South Carolina at an interesting point in their social history. Sometime around 700 to 800 A.D., the earliest signs of the Mississippian culture, known for their large mounds, dependence on corn agriculture and their hierarchically organized societies, were appearing in the Cairo Lowlands of southeastern Missouri. The culture began spreading eastward through a combination of populations moving and indigenous peoples adaptation to the new cultural and social forms.[27] By 1000 A.D., that culture had made its way to the Upper Tennessee Valley and northwestern and central Georgia. It took until 1100 A.D. for the Mississippian culture to reach the Appalachian Highlands and the Savannah River, and another 50 to 100 years for it to make it to the Wateree and Pee Dee Rivers.[28]

That culture was far different from the egalitarian societies which had existed in the Southeast up to that point. Still, the Pee Dee, who were later to show a consistent desire to work with their neighbors, opted to adopt some aspects and at least the appearance of the Mississippian culture rather than resist totally. It was a stance they would take with the Europeans hundreds of years later, adopting European lifestyles while maintaining and closely guarding and, hiding their own culture from outside eyes.

Agriculture played a role in the integration of diverse Native Americans into tribes. Where the tribes located or bill villages was in large part determined by the availability of good farmland and in a bountiful supply of fish. An essential aspect of the Mississippian culture was corn agriculture. While the Native Americans had cultivated corn on a small scale for several centuries as the production of corn began on a larger scale, populations necessarily increased to provide much needed workers. As the populations of the tribes increased, so did their dependence on corn.[29] This new food source resulted in changes to the health of the Mississippians that can be found by examining their bones and teeth.

The cultivation of corn draws heavily on the nutrients of the soil and requires a heavy investment of labor to enjoy a high crop yield. This meant that the tribe had to use extremely rich soils, such as bottom land near the Pee Dee River, and had to labor long and hard in preparing the fields, hoeing weeds, and keeping birds and vermin away until the corn was harvested and then protecting the harvest afterward. All of this labor required a more "structured" society to better organize and control the needed workers.

Most tribes influenced by the Mississippian culture changed to this more centralized government and social structure. The change to this more centralized government and social structure resulted in allegiances to chiefs of larger groups of people rather than the chief among the tribe's kinsmen. People began to regard the chiefs, who could be male or female and still traced their descent matrilineally, and their kinsmen as descendants of the sun, making them divine and set apart from the common people. [30] The building of larger mounds, sometimes in several levels, began as a way to reinforce this separation by setting the chief and family literally above the rest of the tribe. [31]

Such organized chiefdoms could then muster the military muscle to defeat smaller tribes. This led to a rapid spread of the Mississippian culture throughout the southeast. By 1300, bands of the Pee Dee had moved into the Town Creek area, where they built a small substructure mound and ceremonial center and put a palisade around the center to keep the displaced populations out. That move would be the northern-most advancement of the Pee Dee in North Carolina.[32]

So by the time the Pee Dee had their first contact with the Spanish, meeting explorer D'Ailyon in 1521, they had already learned much of the Mississippian ways. But while the Mississippian culture had had an impact on tribal agriculture, pottery- making styles and the implements of warfare, it had not consumed the previous culture as it had the cultures of other tribes.

The meeting with D'Ailyon proved deadly, as European diseases such as smallpox reduced the tribe from a dominant force in the area to a small people located primarily in its present location. By the time Hernando de Soto would reach the area 20 years later, the Vehidi would be a secondary chiefdom within the larger Mississippian-style chiefdom of Cofitachequi.

The tribe at that point had a large city, marked by a series of mounds throughout the area and protected by a "snake" mound more than two miles long. This city, although on the opposite side of the river from the generally accepted location of the city of Ilapi, may in fact have been that city. In fact, in a recent article, noted archaeologist David G. Anderson did in fact place the location of Ilapi on the east side of the Great Pee Dee River.

De Soto had been a captain under Cortez during the conquest of Mexico in 1519. He was searching for gold and was not really interested in colonizing the Southeast. It was his quest for gold that brought de Soto to Cofitachequi located in what is now known as South Carolina. There he encountered the Lady of Cofitachequi. She was a "cacica" or the female chief. The issue of gender equality is addressed elsewhere in this paper.

During his time in Cofitachequi,, de Soto profaned the temple mound at Town Creek. He rode his horse up onto the ceremonial platform on the mound.

The Lady of Cofitachequi bribed de Soto with gifts to spare her village. Despite this, she was taken captive by de Soto, but escaped and returned to her village. Her bribery tactic worked and her village was spared for another 130 years.

African slaves, brought by the Spanish, were apparently the first to call the tribe Pee Dee instead of Vehidi, its name for itself, and told their captors the name meant "Snake People" because the Pee Dee tattooed themselves with snakes and considered them sacred. The snake mound, or the place of the snake, may have also impacted the slaves calling the tribe Snake People. Their use of "Pee Dee," therefore, could have come from the last syllables of Ilapi and Vehidi. Thus the people of the place of the snake became Snake People.

Regardless, the site was clearly special to the Pee Dee. Two centuries later, although the city was no longer used as a ceremonial site, the tribe would threaten war with the English settlers who tried to take this "Old Field."

Francisco Gordillo was the first European to visit the present day South Carolina in 1521. The Spanish attempted the first European settlement near present day Georgetown in 1526, but it failed after 9 months.

In February, 1562, two vessels departed from Le Harve on the northern coast of France. These ships, commanded by Jean Ribault, a Huguenot, were bound for Spanish Florida. In late April, Ribault sighted the east coast of Florida, somewhere in the vicinity of Anastasia Island. On May first, his ships entered the St. Johns River near modern Jacksonville, Florida. After a brief stopover, the two vessels reached Port Royal Sound on the southern coast of South Carolina in mid-May, 1562. A month later, Ribault was on his way back to France, but he left behind 27 men in a small outpost called Charlesfort, somewhere in Port Royal Sound. That outpost was occupied for less than a year before those left in it returned to France.

Upon learning of these attempted French settlements in a land long considered by the Spanish Crown to be Spanish territory, Philip II dispatched Pedro Menéndez de Avilés to Florida to deal with this French intrusion. Menéndez killed or captured nearly all of the few hundred Frenchmen then residing in Fort Caroline.

Upon his arrival, Menéndez established a small outpost at St. Augustine on the Atlantic coast of Florida to serve as a base for operations against the French. Following his defeat of the Frenchmen, Menéndez strengthened the defenses at St. Augustine against counter attack; he then established several other military outposts on both sides of the Florida peninsula and up the Georgia coast.

In January, 1566, Menéndez received a report that the Frenchmen were going to attempt to establish another settlement in Florida, so he gathered a fleet of ships and sailed north from St. Augustine to counter that effort. He did not encounter any sign of French presence on this trip, but he decided to establish an outpost on present-day Parris Island near Beaufort, South Carolina.

He chose this spot because Ribault's initial settlement in Florida had been on or near Parris Island in 1562-1563, and he was concerned that the Frenchmen might return to that same area. Thus Santa Elena became the second of the "two or three towns" Menéndez had agreed to establish in Florida under his contract agreement with Phillip II.

Menéndez' outpost at Santa Elena consisted of a small fort, Fort San Salvador (the location of this fort is currently unknown), with a garrison of about 80 men. In late summer, 1566, Captain Juan Pardo arrived at Santa Elena with an additional force of 250 men, necessitating construction of a larger fort, Fort San Felipe. In December, 1566, Captain Pardo and 125 of his men were sent inland on an expedition intended to establish friendly relations with interior Indians and ultimately to find an overland route to Mexico. This was to be the first of two Pardo expeditions inland in 1566-1568; neither of Pardo's expeditions reached beyond the Appalachian Mountains.

In his contract with Phillip II, Pedro Menéndez had agreed to bring 100 farmers among those in his initial expeditionary force, and he was also obligated to bring an additional 400 settlers to Florida within three years of his arrival. He began settling civilian farmers and artisans at Santa Elena in 1568, and by August, 1569, there were nearly 200 settlers living there in a community composed of about 40 houses; the town was controlled by an organized city government.

Jesuit missionaries worked to convert the Indians around Santa Elena to Catholicism beginning in 1569. Disease epidemics plagued the Santa Elena colonists during their first years, with major outbreaks occurring in 1570 and 1571. Supply ships arrived at irregular intervals, and there were times when both settlers and soldiers suffered greatly as a result. Short supplies caused the residents of Santa Elena to turn to local Indians for help, and before long the Indians were in revolt due to ever increasing demands for food by the Spanish. Part of the garrison of Fort San Felipe was withdrawn by Menéndez in 1570, but it was subsequently reinforced to full strength.

While Menéndez' first settlement was at St. Augustine, he soon made Santa Elena his capital in Florida. When his wife and her attendants arrived in July 1571, they settled at Santa Elena. Santa Elena was a small, struggling community with a total population of 179 settlers and 76 soldiers in August, 1572.

Settlers were primarily farmers, who by this time were growing a variety of crops including corn, squash, melons, barley, and grapes; livestock, including hogs and cattle, as well as chickens, had been introduced and were being raised with limited success.

During Menéndez' absence, Don Diego de Velasco, one of Pedro Menéndez' two sons-in-law and Lieutenant Governor, served as interim governor; he continued in that position following Menéndez' death. During the years that Velasco served as interim governor, he had several run-ins with settlers, and he mistreated the Indians residing in the vicinity of Santa Elena. This poor relationship with the Indians led to a series of attacks on Santa Elena. The loss of thirty soldiers in these attacks ultimately forced the abandonment of the fort and town at Santa Elena in late summer, 1576. As the soldiers and settlers waited to cross the bar in departing Port Royal Sound, they were able to see the town and fort being burned by Indians.[33]

Chapter 4: The Pee Dee and the Colonial Period

In 1663, English King Charles II, who gave away vast regions as if they had really belonged to him, granted to eight of his favorites, the Lords Proprietors[34], a charter and certain privileges, to repay them for their loyalty in restoring him to the throne of his father. This grant was of the territory extending from the present southern line of Virginia to the St. Johns, in Florida, and from the Atlantic to the Pacific. This region was later (1665) extended to include the Albemarle settlers who had moved south from Virginia.

From the inception of South Carolina in 1670 as the Charles Town settlement, land surveys have played a large part in the development of the land into the state as we know it today. Since the first settlement of Charles Town to the final demarcation of the boundary between South Carolina and North Carolina in 1813, surveys (or lack thereof) have guided the path of South Carolina. John Locke, the famous philosopher and economist, had established a plan of government and land settlement for the new colony. Proper land surveying, mapping, and disbursement were crucial parts of his plan.

In order to be granted territory in South Carolina, the Lord Proprietors required extensive surveys for any settler to be granted a parcel of land. This system would last for over 40 years, with colonial surveyors working out of Charles Town. Settlers could obtain land only after going through a rigorous process; they were required to first appear before the governor and the Council, then the governor would issue a warrant, and that warrant would then be taken to a secretary who recorded it. And this was before the surveyors even got involved.

Once the warrant was officially recorded, the surveyor was sent out to make a plat of the land. Once the plat was drawn up, the settler would then have to take said plat back to the secretary to be certified, and a sealed grant would have to be taken back to the governor and council for signatures, and finally, the land grant was made official, and recorded in the register. Because of the lengthy and complicated process, the office of the surveyor general quickly became overrun with eager settlers and inundated with requests.[35]

The first permanent settlement, at Charles Town (Charleston) on the Ashley River, was established by the English in 1670. The first colonists from England began arriving in Charleston in 1670. Like they had the Spanish and Virginians before them, the Pee Dee welcomed this latest group of immigrants. The Pee Dee at this time were living on the Pee Dee River in what would become Marlboro, Chesterfield, Dillon, Florence and Marion Counties in South Carolina, and Richmond and Scotland Counties in North Carolina [36] and had apparently returned to their old habit of living in small communities and villages rather than at one large site. Mooney estimated the number of Pee Dee as 600 in 1600. [37]

By this time, the tribe had already established trade with the Virginia settlements and was also working well with its nearest neighbors, having a close association with the Winyah and Waccamaw tribes. [38] They would continue with the English their long-held tradition of finding ways to work with their neighbors and form mutually profitable relationships revolving around the fur trade. In doing so they avoided much of the Indian slave trade that developed in the Carolinas. [39]

Native American slavery was also practiced by the English in the Carolinas who sold Native American captives into slavery on the English plantations in the Caribbean. One of the first tribes that specialized in slave raids and trade with Carolina was the Westo, followed by many others including the Yamassee, Chickasaw, and Creek. Historian Alan Gallay estimates the number of Native Americans in southeast America sold in the British slave trade from 1670-1715 as between 24,000 and 51,000. He also notes that during this period more slaves (Native American, African, or otherwise) were exported from Charleston than imported.[40]

The southern colonies relied on slave labor to cultivate the cash crops raised on large plantations. They were unable to use Native Americans as slaves because they were in familiar territory and could easily escape into the countryside. So enslaved Native Americans were exported to the Caribbean with African slaves were imported.

The first African slave ships reached the colonies in the 1620s, and by the end of the century, the slave trade between West Africa and the southern colonies was thriving. In the half century before 1715, intertribal warfare, kidnapping, and enslavement displaced thousands and reshaped the lives of all of the region's inhabitants. Disparate Indian communities formed powerful confederacies in an effort to take advantage of the lucrative trade and avoid enslavement. By exporting their human cargoes everywhere from Boston to Barbados, the British slave traders of South Carolina spurred the colony's economy while extending its influence among slave-hunting Indians as far west as the Mississippi River. No corner of the region escaped the hunt for slaves or its consequences.

The general outlines of this trade are no secret, but the mystery remains in the significance of the details. Because no colonial power compiled records on the illicit trade, historians have been reluctant to reconstruct this complicated story from disparate and patchy sources. One of the greatest thefts of people in North American history has been left largely untold.[41]

This represented a commerce that flourished from 1670, when the English founded South Carolina, through 1717, when they concluded peace with the pan-Indian alliance that nearly destroyed them. South Carolina's emergent planter class exported Indians to finance the purchase of African slaves. Upon the backs of African laborers who were less likely than Indian chattel to run away or revolt, White Carolinians would construct a more lucrative (and, to their minds, respectable) economy based on rice and indigo.

Despite the Spaniards' century-long head start and Carolinians' internecine feuding, the later arrivals quickly proved more ruthless and effective at colonizing the region. The English and the nascent Indian confederacies realized that cooperation would best serve their respective interests. At the heart of this cooperation lay the slave trade. Carolina's proprietary sponsors in England tried to limit trade with Native Americans, but ambitious colonists ignored these distant overseers and quickly "infected" the South with this highly profitable traffic.

The English did not act alone. Indians traded to avoid enslavement themselves and because the sale of slaves enabled them to acquire large amounts of the cloth, beads, and guns that Carolinians offered in return.

In the five years following the outbreak of the War of Spanish Succession in 1701, Carolinians advanced their economic and military fortunes by enlisting native allies to conduct massive raids that destroyed Florida's missions and threatened the stability of newly established French Louisiana. French officials responded by encouraging their own allies to capture slaves, and French and Spaniards together tried to use their Indian allies for colonial defense and a fruitless counterattack against Charles Town.

Bitter squabbles among rival traders made a mockery of any regulatory efforts, and as traders continued to beat, rape, cheat, and occasionally enslave their Indian allies, Indian disaffection quietly grew. The raids that Carolinians sponsored across the region enabled them to export, according to some calculations, 24,000-51,000 Indians at prices comparable to African slaves.

In 1711 South Carolina's English Colonist's enlisted the Pee Dee's to fight in the Tuscarora War. North Carolina's English settlers had asked for help to put down the uprising of the Tuscarora Indians. There were 500 Indian allies, but what tribes other than the Pee Dee is unknown. In 1711 there were still a number of small tribes in South Carolina, such as the Waccamaw, Santee, Catawba, Wateree, and the Edisto. The Pee Dee fought alongside the South Carolina Colonists in the Yamassee War of 1715-1716. The defeated Yamassee returned to Spanish Florida.

In 1715, Native Americans throughout the region abruptly halted this commerce when they simultaneously killed the English traders among them and began raiding the colony itself. When the Yamassee War of 1715-17 ended, the Carolinians' plantations, trade, and regional influence lay in ruins.

The end of hostilities marked not just the demise of the slave trade, but a new watershed. Carolinian involvement in a staple-crop economy dependent on African slaves began in earnest after 1717; this new economic system would define White wealth until the Civil War.[42]

The social and legal relations between the English colonists and the African slaves were governed by racial beliefs and economics. Since the first meetings of West Africans and Europeans, Europeans had judged Africans to be their cultural inferiors. This belief shaped the slave codes that the colonies began to enact in the late seventeenth century. Africans were human chattel with no civil rights.

The South Carolina Slave Code of 1740 reflected concerns about controlling slaves. Section X authorized a White person to detain and examine any slave found outside a house or plantation who was not accompanied by a White person. Section XXXVI prohibited slaves from leaving their plantation, especially on Saturday nights, Sundays, and holidays. Slaves who violated the law could be subjected to a "moderate whipping." Section XLV prohibited White persons from teaching slaves to read and write.

Criminal behavior by slaves, especially actions directed against White persons, was severely punished under the code. Section IX provided that in the case of a capital crime, a slave must be brought to trial in a summary proceeding within three days of apprehension. Under section XVII, the killing of a White person by a slave was a capital crime, but section XXXVII treated a White person who killed a slave quite differently. Willful murder of a slave was punished by a fine of 700 pounds. Killing a slave "on a sudden heat of passion" resulted in a fine of 350 pounds.

The code did recognize that slaves were entitled to a sufficient level of food, clothing, and shelter. Section XXXVIII permitted a complaint to be filed against a slave owner who was derelict in providing the necessities. A court could order the owner to provide relief to the slaves. Likewise, section XLIV authorized the fining of slave owners who worked their slaves more than fifteen hours a day during the hottest time of the year.

Within four years of their arrival in Charleston, the colonial government sent Captain Maurice Matthews, William Owen and John Boone to make a treaty with those he called the Esaw or Esau Indians. He described these Indians as living to the east of the Catawba on the North Carolina line. Because this aptly describes the territory of the Pee Dee, the group could have mistakenly been referring to the Pee Dee as Esau because of their similar language base. While it is clear the Pee Dee are not the Esau, this could be the first treaty between the English and the Pee Dee.

The Carolinas resisted British rule early in their history. In 1693 the colony won the right to initiate legislation in the British House of Commons. Bath, near the mouth of the Pamlico River, was the first town to be incorporated (1706).

An Englishman born in London, named John Lawson, "built a house" as he tells us in his book, "A New Voyage to Carolina," in the spring of 1701 on what is now called Lawson's creek, "about half a mile from an Indian town" (Chattooka) "at the fork of Neuse river" – in the fork of Neuse river and Trent river – "where I dwelt by myself, excepting a young Indian fellow, and a bulldog that I had along with me."[43]

Lawson lived in that house most of the time until the 6th of January 1709, when he sailed for England, and he may have been the only non-Indian living on Neuse River during all that time.   But then in 1710 Lawson arranged a sale, by the Neusiok Indians, of the site of Chattooka to the English, hereby establishing the present city of New Bern, N.C.   No White settlers lived in 1712 anywhere in between New Bern and John Lane (a settler living near the present Oatland, S.C.). Settlement spread from Charles Town south toward Beaufort (founded 1710), north toward Georgetown (1735), and inland along the rivers.   Political strife and Indian wars slowed the Carolina Colony's growth, however, and as "Charles Town" grew more rapidly; the territory began to be known as North and South Carolina.

Chapter 5: Pee Dee References in Colonial Records

It is clear that the Pee Dee were allies of the colonial government by 1711. In that year, several of the Pee Dee men fight in Capt. Bull's "Esaw Company" in the Tuscarora War.[44] In a letter dated February 14th, 1711, Barnwell mentions that he had marched eight days from the Pee Dee River to the Cape Fear River and had ordered during the sixty day march that Captain John Bull make another circuit among his Indians and meet him back at the river. Bull brought about 200 men, some whom were bowmen because they had no guns, and some whom were Pee Dee. According to Barnwell's own count, after many desertions, he had 18 Pee Dee men and 42 Cheraws.[45]

In fact, the earliest written English record of the Pee Dee is found in a map which shows "Colonel Barnwell's Course 1711." His course follows the north bank of "Peedee River," from the "Sarraw" (another Indian nation) to the "Peedee" (Indian nation). He most likely followed an existing Indian path down the east side of Great Pee Dee River, from present-day Wallace, S.C. to Pee Dee, S.C. Most of the path runs through present-day Marlboro County, entering the northeastern corner of Marion County just before reaching Pee Dee. The path leads to the Great Pee Dee river from the "Waxaws" (the Waxhaw or Flathead Indians) on Catawba river; crosses the Great Pee Dee to get to the Sarraw Indians on the other side; runs alongside the Great Pee Dee to the town of the Peedee Indians (about 45 miles from the Sarraw town); and veers off in a northeastward direction to "Scavan 30" on the Little Pee Dee river in present-day Dillon county, S.C.

Barnwell describes the area as being "Good Land, large Timber," and the way from Little Pee Dee River to the Cape Fear River as going through "Low Level Pine Land full of Swamps." He probably crossed the Lumber River near present-day Pembroke, N.C. Colonial records show that no European settlers lived between the Santee River and Neuse River in 1712, other than for possibly five families a few miles to the north of Santee River. The two rivers enter the Atlantic Ocean full 200 miles, by air, distant from each other.

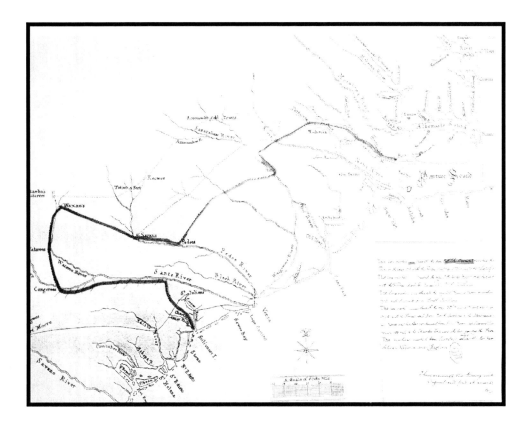

There is no detailed information on the part that the Peedees played in the massive Indian uprising against the colony of South Carolina, known as the Yamassee War, beyond that sometime in 1716 after the 15th of May and well before the 10th of July, "the Wawees, Wackamaws, Peedees and others came down and concluded a peace with this government." Or by another account, "the Waccamaws and those other nations bordering on the sea shore to the northward, the Sarraws excepted ... made peace with us, fearing the Cherokees." The reason for their fear: "the Charakee... have done us a signal piece of service, in compelling the Catawbas and those other small nations about them to make peace with us, whom otherwise they threatened to destroy."

Getting back to the Keyauwse, Waccamaw, Peedee and Winia ("the Wawees, Wackamaws, Peadees and others"): "The conditions of peace agreed upon with them, is that they shall deliver up all belonging to the White people, and that they shall use their endeavors to destroy the Sarraws." That would be the Saraw Indians and among them, the Saxapahaw and Waxhaw or Flathead Indians.[46]

The Pee Dee had fought alongside the colonists in the Yamassee War from 1715 through 1716; the war took a terrible toll on the tribe, and British records show that the tribe had been utterly eliminated in the conflict.[47] It is apparent, however, that news of their demise had been greatly exaggerated, with several survivors heading back to the Marlboro County area. [48]

The "Peedee Indians in general, and a Peedee Indian man named Westoe (Anglicized to "Tom West") as seen in the journal of the Commissioners of the Indian Trade from the summer of 1716 to the summer of 1717.

"Mr. Watis, Sr., "according to a former order informed us that Saukey is a more proper and convenient place for settling a factory" (factor's, or trade middleman's, headquarters) "and trading house at, than the old Caseka's on Black river, for a commerce with the Peedees and Waccamaw Indians."

During the early eighteenth century, the fur trade, especially in deerskins, was an important commercial activity in the Carolinas. The fur trade in the southern colonies was established around 1670 based on the export hub of Charleston, South Carolina. Word spread amongst Native American hunters that the Europeans would exchange pelts for European-manufactured goods that were highly desired in native communities. Axe heads, knives, awls, fish hooks, cloth of various type and color, woolen blankets, linen shirts, kettles, jewelry, glass beads, muskets, ammunition and powder were some of the major items exchanged on a 'per pelt' basis.

Colonial trading posts in the southern colonies also introduced many types of alcohol (especially brandy and rum) for trade. European traders flocked to the continent and made huge profits off the exchange. A metal axe head, for example, was exchanged for one beaver pelt (also called a 'beaver blanket'). The same pelt could fetch enough to buy dozens of axe heads in England, making the fur trade extremely profitable for the European nations. The iron axe heads replaced stone axe heads which the natives made by hand in a labor-intensive process, so they derived substantial benefits from the trade as well.

Often, the political benefits of the fur trade became more important than the economic aspects. Trade was a way to forge alliances and maintain good relations between different cultures. The fur traders, men of social and financial standing, usually went to North America as young single men and used marriages as the currency of diplomatic ties, marriages and relationships between Europeans and First Nations/Native Americans became common. Traders often married or cohabited with high-ranking Indian women. Fur trappers and other workers usually had relationships with lower ranking women.

Because of the wealth at stake, different European-American governments competed with each other for control of the fur trade with the various native societies. Native indigenous peoples of the Americas sometimes based decisions of which side to support in time of war upon which side provided them with the best trade goods in an honest manner. Because trade was so politically important, it was often heavily regulated in hopes (often futile) of preventing abuse. Unscrupulous traders sometimes cheated natives by plying them with alcohol during the transaction, which subsequently aroused resentment and often resulted in violence. [49]

William Waties stayed at Saukey as a fur trader among the Peedee Indians during most of the month of August 1716, but no longer. He and one assistant would have been the only non-Indians up there, and indeed the only Whites anywhere around other than for your occasional unlicensed trader. The northern frontier of White settlement lay 50 miles to the south by air, at "Wineau."

Westoe is the first individual member of the Peedee tribe of whom we hear. Although Mr. Waties (who could speak Peedee, but not Woccon, or Waccamaw, as of the previous April) had shifted his base of operations, for the first time, from the Peedee nation to the Waccamaw nation, he still kept one associate from the Peedee tribe – Westoe – in his employ.

"At a Council held the l2th September 1717. Mr. Hughes came with about fifteen Indians of several nations (as Peedees, Waccamaws, Wynmays, Cape Fears, and Waywees). And Mr. Hughes told the Governor that they were come to renew their old friendship. And the Indians layed down their old commissions end desired to have new for them, and to have new articles signed between them..."[50]

At a meeting with the Indian Trade Commissioners: "Indian Kings (Johnny, Gary, the Waywee Captain, and several of the Chief Men of the Waccamaws and Wineaus, and one Peedee Indian) cane and appeared before the Board. And informed that, having paid their submissions to the Governor, they desired to be heard about matters of trade.

"Thereupon being asked concerning the same, the Waccamaws and Wineaus proposed to have a Trading House settled at Black River, as being the most safe place. But the Peedee man declared that his people preferred there to any other place for trade; but however if the Trading House should be settled at Black River, they would come down thither.

14th of September 1717. "‥ And on the 14th day of said September, articles of alliance was renewed by the said parties, and new Commissions given to several of the said Nations."[51]

These "Commissions" were handwritten parchments, only one copy of each, drawn up on the finest and most durable high rag content paper, with calligraphic flourishes penned with a quill and large red wax Seals for signatures. The colonial government of South Carolina issued them in recognition of any new chief, headman. King or war captain among the Indians, hiving one made up for the Indian who had just attained office. In the decade 1732-1742, South Carolina issued some sixty of these Indian Commissions to headmen and so on among the Catawba, Cherokee, Cape Fear, Kusso, Saraw, Eno, New Windsor Chickasaw, Wateree, Peedee and Upper Creek Indians, issuing none at all, on the average, about every other calendar year. Though the Indians could not read these inscribed parchments, they accepted and kept them nevertheless, and sometimes asked for them or (as in the case of the Catawbas in 1755) for replacements for old copies made unreadable by being carried about in the rain.[52]

In October or November of 1735 the frontier jumped as much as twenty-seven miles into the interior — farther than that by water — with the founding of the present Kingstree, S.C. by possibly ten families of Irish immigrants just off the boat from Belfast. They called the new settlement "Williamsburg" for the first two or three years. It lay fifty miles or so northeast of the Winia Indians (considered a tribe of "settlement Indians") and forty miles southeast of the Peedee Indians (still a separate nation of people').

In 1737, the tribe petitioned South Carolina for a parcel of land to live upon. They, along with the Notchees, were moved to a 100 acre reservation provided by James Coachman in 1738. This reservation was in Berkeley County, along the Edisto River.[53]

25th March 1738.   William Bull.

May it please your Honor?

In answer to your message just now communicated to this House, we take the liberty to acquaint your Honor that we have agreed that the shot of land containing 100 acres mentioned in the said message, shall be bought for the use of the PeDee & Notchee Indians, and that the sum to be paid for the same, shall be provided for in the next year's estimate.

We also desire your Honor will be pleased to take such proper measures in that respect, that the said land may be secured and conveyed to trustees for the use of the said Indians.

By order of the house

Charles Pinckney, Speaker

On March 28th, 1738, "The Notchee and Pedee Indians have made application to this government for small quantity of land to be given them to live on.

"... Gabriel Manigault and his heirs shall from time to time and at all times for and during the term of 1000 years to be computed from the date hereof permit and suffer the said Notchee and Peedee Indians, their descendants and offspring, to occupy, possess and enjoy the said piece or parcel of land containing 100 acres..."

An account of Capt. John D. amounting to the sum of £10, it being for cash given to the PeDee Indians who went down to Pon Pon with Capt. James Coachman in pursuit of the rebellious Negroes, which account having been read also to the House, it was ordered that the same be referred to the consideration of the Committee On Petitions & Accounts.[54]

March 6th, 1742

"A Special Commission / on Parchment / for King Will, King of the Peedees over the four Hole Swamp... in the Room of Long Will."[55]

That same day, the Secretary of the Province spent a pound and ten shillings (a pound and a half) to have drawn up another parchment similarly bestowing the recognition of the colonial government upon "Johnny, Chief Captain under King Will."[56] King Will and his "Chief Captain", whatever the names the two men possessed in their own language,[57] got to keep their respective parchments.[58] (The Peedee Indian nation had lived entirely on Great Pee Dee river until 1757, when they and the Saraw Indians had sold their land there[59], the Peedee Indians acquiring a hundred-acre Natchez-Peedee reservation, as one might term it, on Edisto river's Indian Field Swamp.[60] But between 1740 and 1742 the Peedee Indians apparently left that reservation[61] to settle part on Four Hole Swamp and part[62] on Santee River.)[63]

A well-known trader who himself had a half-Catawba son 14 years of age,[64] wrote the following letter (datelined "SaxeGotha Township the 23rd July 1744")[65] to South Carolina*s Governor James Glen;[66]

"May it please your Excellency –

"I received advice yesterday night by some people trapping (which was confirmed by an escaped Catawba Indian), that:

"Twelve men of the Catawba Indians, going down to renew the friendship with the Pedees and Kotchees" (Natchez) "living within the" (English) "settlements – they met the 16th or 17th instant" (on the 16th or 17th of July 1744) "the said Pedees and Kotchees in a body at Mr. Fuller's Cowpen about the Four Holes Swamp, where there is a store and tavern kept by one Williams, or William Patten.

"Where the Catawbas getting strong liquor" (from the store) "and being drunk, the Notchees assaulted them and killed ten of them, so is that but two and some women escaped.

"Amongst them there is one Captain Jack killed, who had a Captain's Commission from this Government" (dated April 29th, 1741, calling him 'Captain Jack of Soutry Town'), "and was a beloved man and reputed warrior amongst the Catawbas." [67]

Governor Glen dictated a letter:

I have just received information of an unlucky accident which happened about a week ago at or near the store belonging to the late Major Fuller, somewhere about the Four Holes, where some Notchee Indians have fallen upon and killed five or six of the Catawbas, being instigated thereto by a White person who keeps that store" (and whom Glen would later identify as 'one Patteraw, Irishman'). [68]

"The Catawbas, as I understand, have already set out to take their revenge. Which has obliged the Notchees and Peedees to come further down amongst the settlements," the landholdings of the English colonists, "for protection.....? I hear they are at Mr. Beard's plantation, in the neighborhood" (the neighborhood in which did then live "the Honorable William Middleton, Esquire," the man to whom Governor Glen wrote). [69]

Relations between the two tribes continued to be strained following the murders, and in 1746, the Pee Dee considered withdrawing from the Catawba confederacy. South Carolina Governor James Glen convinced the tribe, using a ramrod demonstration borrowed from the Six Nations of the Iroquois, that there is strength in the unity of the tribes.

Like the Six Nations, who showed one arrow could be broken easily but several arrows together could not be broken, Glen showed that ramrods together were unbreakable. The Pee Dee decided to remain in the confederacy, but also chose to continue to have their own "king."[70]

That the Pee Dee owned slaves is without question, for it is during this time period, from August 30 to September 6, 1748, that the following notice appeared in the South Carolina Gazette: "Taken up by Michael Welch, overseer to the Subscriber, on an Island called Uchee Island, a Negro fellow, who gives the following account of himself, viz, that he belonged formerly to Mr. Fuller, and was sold by him to Billy, King of the Pedee Indians; that the Catawba Indians took him from King Billy, and carried him to their nation; and in endeavoring to make his escape from the Catawbas, he was lost in the woods, and had been so a considerable time before he was taken. He is a middle-sized fellow, and a little pot-bellied; says his name is Fortune, but is suspected to have another name which he does not care to own. Any person having any right or property in the said Fellow may apply to the subscriber, now in Charlestown. Isaac Marksdale"[71]

At least one primary item of importance can be gleaned from this reference. As late as 1748, when the Pee Dee were already reputed to have been absorbed by the Catawba, they were living at enough distance from the Catawba that a slave could be said to be taken from one nation up to another .

The South Carolina Gazette reported a visit to Charleston of eleven chiefs of the Catawba and Cheraw in July, 1739. The Cheraw, however, did not altogether favor their residence among the Catawba, and scattered bands of the former remained eastward near the settlements. The Gazette carried the news on June 2, 1746, that Governor Glen of South Carolina had in April met a delegation of Catawba Indians on the Santee River near the Congaree. T here a trader among the Catawba, named Brown, informed the Governor that some of the "Pedees and Cheraws (two small tribes who have long been incorporated with the Catawbas), intended to leave them, which might prove of dangerous conscience at a time when they were so closely attacked by their enemies, the Northern Indians." The Governor's conference proceeded in the following manner:

"The governor ordered the rammers of all the pistols which he had delivered to the Indians to be laid upon the table, desiring that such as were Pedees and Charaws might advance, and they, being in a body near him, he spoke to them in these words: "It gives me great concern, my friends, to hear that you entertain the least thought of leaving the Catawbas, with whom you have been so long and so closely united. This union makes you strong, and enables you to defend yourselves and annoy our enemies; but should you ever separate, you would thereby weaken yourselves, and be exposed to every danger. Consider that if you were single and divided, you may be broke as easily as I break this stick" (at the same time breaking one of the rammers); "but if you continue united together, and stand by one another, it will be as impossible to hurt or break you, as it is impossible for me to break these, (his Excellency then taking up a handful of rammers). After this they all promised to continue together in their camp.[72]

An altercation in 1744 between youths of the Catawba and Pee Dee tribes led to the Catawba forcing the Pee Dee off of their lands and back into White settlements. South Carolina referred to Indians living within the colony's settled areas as "Settlement Indians", and a 1740s list of such tribes included the Pee Dee. Additionally, in 1752 the Catawba asked South Carolina to encourage the Pee Dee "Settlement Indians" to move north and rejoin the Catawba.

Many tribes, including the Pee Dee, developed a relationship of accommodation with the colonies that persisted through the early 18th century. They served as a kind of police and security force in exchange for trade goods, weapons, and money. The colonies paid for "vermin" such as wolves, "tigers" (cougars), and bears. They also hunted game animals and sold the meat to colonists. But their chief service was in capturing runaway slaves.

South Carolina worked to encourage Indian hostility toward Africans, and African fear of Indians. A series of laws were passed that rewarded Indians for capturing runaway slaves and absolved them of responsibility if runaways were killed in the process. In contrast, Africans suffered punishment and severe penalties for attacking Indians. As late as 1750, reportedly more than 400 "ancient native" (or Settlement Indians) lived within South Carolina, with their "chief service" being "hunting Game, destroying Vermin and Beasts of Prey, and in capturing Runaway slaves."[73]

By the 1750s, Germans and Scottish-Irish from Pennsylvania and Virginia were settling the Piedmont (present day SC) on small, subsistence farms in contrast to the coastal plantations.[74]

Not much is heard from the tribe until 1751, and it can be assumed that the three separate Pee Dee settlements (Marlboro-Marion (now Dillon) Co., Santee at the Black River and at Four Holes) were living in relative peace with the Catawba. In 1751, Governor James Glen wrote in a letter to Governor Clinton of New York that the Pee Dee were living in peace with both the Indians and Whites of South Carolina.[75]

In another letter that year, written November 12, 1751 to the Six Nations of the Iroquois Confederacy, Governor Glen urges the Six Nations to make peace with the Pee Dee and the Catawba.[76] There is no record of whether the Six Nations responded, but there does not seem to be major conflict between the two confederacies after that point.

King Hagler of the Catawba sent a letter dated November 21, 1752 to Governor James Glen saying a great many Pee Dee were living in the White settlements. Hagler asked Glen to ask those Pee Dee to move up and join with the Catawba.[77]

By the mid-1750s, the Pee Dee were divided into at least three bands, one in the Marlboro-Marion County area, one in the Santee area and another among the Edisto Indians. Each band maintained their own king."[78] According to the Indian Book, Vol. V, Lewis John (or Lewis Jones) was made "king" over all the Pee Dee during this time period.[79]

18th of April 1755. "Mr. Bond (from the committee appointed to consider of proper "rays for establishing rangers on the Northern Frontiers of this province) made the following report", consisting of six recommendations:"First, that two companies of rangers under the command of two captains, and fifteen men each, be established and immediately raised... Sixthly, and that it be an instruction to the Captains of the Rangers to observe the behavior of the Pedee and Waccamaw Indians. And in case of an alarm, to direct them to repair within the settlements to such place as shall be appointed them."[80]

In 1755, perhaps in response to King Hagler's letter three years earlier, some of the Pee Dee tribe moved over to join the Catawba. Others joined with the "Lumber River Indians."[81] Still others were listed in a settlement at Goose Creek while more remained in the Marlboro County area.

It is clear that during this period, Lewis John (or Jones) is living on his land grant on the Black River, but letters from John Evans to the Governor make it equally clear that he moved easily between the communities and is accepted as chief by them.

In 1755, John Evans was sent by Governor Glen to investigate the killing and scalping of two Pee Dee women in the Goose Creek area and the capture of several Pee Dee boys. Catawbas are suspected.[82] King Hagler denied any involvement by his tribe in the incident.[83] The Pee Dee were considered part of the Catawba confederacy at that time, but in his journal, Evans stated that the camp of the Pee Dee was two days ride from the Catawba.[84] Jones is mentioned as traveling from the Nation in what would become Marlboro County to the settlement of Pee Dee in Georgetown to investigate the incident.

JOURNAL OF JOHN EVANS[85]

His Excellency Governor Glen's Letter to me dated September the 8th, 1755, I received October 5th, 1755, I being but just recovering from a violent Fit of Sickness, was not able to ride or undertake the Journey to the Catawbaw Nation pursuant to his Excellency's Orders until the 14th Instant and then employed one Man to go with me.

The King and Head Men met and desired to know what I was come for. I told them that there was two Pedee Women killed, one scalped, and two Boys carried away from out of the Settlements and it was thought that it was done by some of their Nation and one Notchee which was called the Notchee Doctor. And his Excellency the Governor had sent me to demand the Boys and I then and there demanded those Boys. I further acquainted them that his Excellency the Governor desired that they would not come into the settlements without they were sent for, for the White People might mistake them and do them a Mischief, believing them to be Enemy Indians.

I farther said that it was his Excellency the Governor's Pleasure that the Catawbaw People should not attempt to carry any of the Indians that were now living in the Settlements up to their Nation on any Pretence whatever [95] without his Permission first. There Answer was that old Men should always speak Truth and the most of them were grey headed, and they for their Parts did not hurt the Pedees nor did not know or believe the Mischief was done by any belonging to that Nation, and further said that when the Northward Indians were in their Nation, [they] bound the same three Women and two Men, and the Catawbaws released the three Women but the Northward Indians carried the Men away. I charged the Nation with robbing the Cherrockees by Emelia Township. The Head Men (after some Pause) said that there was eight young Men gone that Way hunting, perhaps they had done it; the King said that before they went out he had given them a great Charge not to trouble the White Women nor do no Harm amongst the White People, and if they had robbed the Cherrockees he would take care that the Cherrockees should have their Goods again.

22d. I set out from the Catawbaw Nation homeward and at Night came to a Camp of Pedees. I acquainted them with my Errand to the Nation and desired them to let me know, if they could, who it was that killed and scalped the Pedee Women and carried the Boys away.

Lewis Jones, their Chief, answered that soon after the Pedees were killed, he went down from the Nation to the Settlements to enquire what Harm was done by Goos Creek, [he met] a free Indian named Prince who lives in the Settlements and Prince told him that a Day or two before the Mischief was done there was five Cherrockees and one Notchee seen to go by Muncks Corner and Lewis John said he did believe they scalped the Women and carried the Boys away.

KING HAGLER TO KING WAITES

Catawba Nation, January 24th, 1756

Yesterday arrived here from the Fort upon New River one White Man and one Cherokee Indian, and brought with them a Letter from the Captain of the said Fort acquainting us that some time ago they were upon the scout a hunting for Enemys [they] came up with nine Indians. The said Indians had two Boys Prisoners with them. They went to make their Escape but the White Men pursued them and killed one of them and lost one of their Men and rescued the two Boys which at first said they were Cherokees but now say they are Catawbas. One of them talks English and calls himself Dick. One of the Boys was wounded but he has got well. They sent for us to come and bring them Home so as the Children is yours we desire you will come and go and fetch them Home and not let us be blamed for that we never did. You may go in seven Days from this Place to where your Children is. We remain your friends and brothers.

Soon after that treaty was concluded at Albany, several Mohawks came to my Nation, and did then catch 2 Chickesaw women and two children, 3 Peedee women and one man, all of whom they brought into my nation. They left the women with me but carried away the man with them, & upon their departure they killed several of my people and took away 2 women prisoners; notwithstanding of which, when the six Mohawks came to my Nation, I would not suffer one of them to be hurt, but treated them well. I returned all the Mohawks, whom I'd taken prisoner before the peace, agreeable to the Treaty. But the Catawbas prisoners with the Mohawks have not been returned.

When that peace was concluded, I very well remember that it was then agreed that if any Nation should attack the English, the Mohawks & Cataawbas should join & assist the English. I had formerly a good many warriors, they are now reduced to a small number, but with those few I will take your Honor by the hand, & fight your enemies.

My skin is dark, the outlook upon myself as a White man. I am very sensible of your goodness in supplying my people with clothing & victuals, and I am thankful for it. I never would receive any clothing from the French and am determined to live and die with the English.[86]

Relations between the tribes must have improved somewhat after the incident, for in Mount Pleasant on August 25, 1759, Lewis John (Or Jones) signed as one of the Catawba headmen on a treaty requesting ammunition. Although he is not listed as Pee Dee on the document, John (or Jones) is still living among his people at Santee at this time. His incorporation on the treaty as a Catawba headman while living among and governing his own tribe makes it clear that the Pee Dee did not move to Catawba.

14th of March 1758. A surveyor drew up the finished plat,' shown below, of five-sixteenths of a square mile on Great Pee Dee river. This was land the Pee Dee Indians still considered that they had never sold, and still owned; and as one of their "old fields" (abandoned village sites).

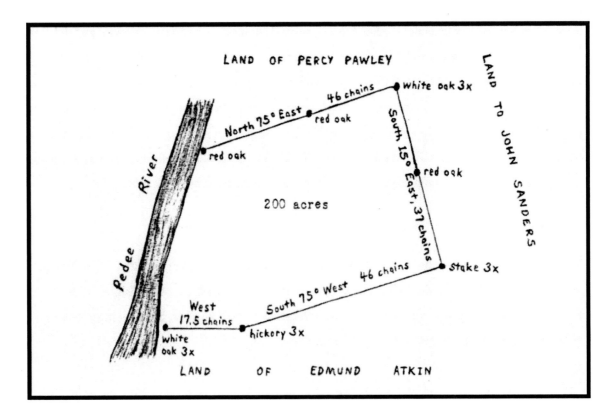

Mentions of the tribe decreased during this time period, although it is clear that the Pee Dee were still in the areas where they had always been living and were still functioning as a tribe. By 1766, individual Pee Dee Indians in all three communities were recognized as landholders on "unrecorded plats for land not granted," the legal designation for inherited land. Yet despite owning their own land, the neighbors of the Pee Dee still recognized that they functioned as a tribe, and continued to use their services to assist the colonial government.

Nearly nine years after that, Governor Glen wrote another letter, this one in reference to the Indian leader spoken of in 1745 as "Robin, Chief Warrior of the Peedees near Four Holes."[87] The Council Journal for that day (April 21st, 1755) duly records that "... The widow of King Robin (a settlement Indian who was killed by some Northern Indians at the Four Hole Swamp) had an order on the Commissary General to furnish her with: A blanket. Six yards of calico and linen for two shifts." [88]

"Mr. Fuller's Cowpen... where there is a store and tavern kept by one Williams, or William Patten," is part of Four Hole Swamp on which one major band of the Peedee Indians lived from 1742 to 1755. We have the same place described as "Fuller's Cowpen" and as "the store belonging to the late Major Fuller."[89] And finally as "the house of one Patteraw – Irishman – who contrary to his duty and the laws of this Province, furnished" the Indians, principally the Catawba delegation, "with rum and punch."[90]

8th of June 1759.   "In the Council Chamber Friday the 8th day of June 1759.

"Mr. John Thompson of Peede attended to answer to the petition of the 16th March past from the Welsh people against him (setting forth the apprehensions they are under, from the Peede and Charraw Indians running amongst their settlements under pretense of hunting; and several other complaints against the said Thompson; and so forth).

"He acknowledged to have purchased from the Charraw and Peedee Indians, about two years since, for a valuable consideration, all their lands upon Peedee River (except two old Fields— one of which is nor- within a plantation settled by Messieurs Laroches; and the other possessed by Thomas Grooms).   In which are about forty old Fields.

But denied that he had sold any part thereof, to the Virginians or any others. Only on condition provided he could obtain grants for the same from the King, he offered to assign over to this Government the conveyance made to him by the Indians, for the same value as he gave them an account of; which he will lay before this Board next week in order to execute the same.

"He said that the demand made by the Indians lately was only for the two above old Fields. For one of which, Mr. Laroche hath satisfied them. That he hath had no hand in promoting any misunderstanding between the Welsh and Indians or Virginians and so on.

"On the contrary, that he will tell the Indians that he hath sold the said lands to the Government. And also that he will satisfy the said Indians that the Welsh are the people who were appointed by the Government to live upon those lands.

"It is the opinion of this Board (in order to prevent disturbance to the new settlers on Peede, and to engage Mr. John Thompson to use his endeavors with the Charraw and other Indians therein) that he be reimbursed the expense he was at in the purchase which he made of the said lands on Peede from those Indians, out of the Township Fund, upon his surrendering to his Majesty the instrument which he hath from those Indians, and making a proper conveyance of the same to this Government."

In the 1760s the regulator movement developed in the country, partially because there were only three justices of the peace. In South Carolina, the Regulator movement was an organized effort by backcountry settlers to restore law and order and establish institutions of local government. Plagued by roving bands of outlaws and angered by the assembly's failure to provide the western counties with courts and petty officers, the leading planters, supported by small farmers, created (1767) an association to regulate backcountry affairs. They brought criminals to justice and set up courts to resolve legal disputes. The assembly and the governor, recognizing the legitimacy of the grievances, did not attempt to crush the movement. By 1768, order was restored, and the Circuit Court Act of 1769, providing six court districts for the backcountry, led the Regulators to disband. Tensions remained, however, between the western farmers and the tidewater aristocracy.[91]

Two factions of the Baptist movement, Regular Baptist and New Light Baptist contended for acceptance among the Indians during this time period. New settlements of small farms began spreading across the countryside. These new settlers faced an established slaveholding class on large plantations.

The new settlers and the plantation owners both looked down upon any person suspected of being mixed blood or mulatto, especially those who chose to live like Indians by hunting and gathering rather than farming. Pee Dee names of the period included Driggers, Grooms, Chavis, and Locklear. This will become clear in subsequent discussion.

Chapter 6: Pee Dee Participation in the American Revolution

Indians fought in the Revolution for Indian liberties and Indian homelands, not for the British Empire. However, the image of Indian participation presented in the Declaration of Independence prevailed: most Americans believed that Indians had backed monarchy and tyranny. A nation conceived in liberty need feel no remorse about dispossessing and expelling those who had fought against its birth.

The Declaration of Independence accused King George III of unleashing "merciless Indian Savages" against innocent men, women, and children. The image of ferocious warriors propelled into action by a tyrannical monarch fixed in memory and imagination the Indians' role in the Revolution and justified their subsequent treatment. Some Indians sided with the Americans, but many Indian Nations tried to stay out of the conflict, and those who fought with the British were not the king's pawns. They allied with the Crown as the best hope of protecting their homelands from the encroachments of American colonists and land speculators. The British government had afforded Indian lands a measure of protection by the Royal Proclamation of 1763 which had attempted to restrict colonial expansion beyond the Appalachian Mountains and had alienated many American colonists. Indians knew that the Revolution was a contest for Indian land as well as for liberty.

"The national mythology accords Indians a minimal and negative role in the story of the Revolution: they chose the wrong side and lost." The reality was much more complex and had lasting implications for the Indians and their eventual fate at the hands of the new American Republic. The American Revolution negatively affected the Indian tribes whether or not they actually fought in the war. The Revolution pitted the Indians against Europeans and often forced them to fight amongst themselves. There is so much diversity that it is impossible to generalize; each Indian group has its own unique ways of thinking, believing, and valuing. With diverse influences shaping each group, they were bound to approach maintaining their independence differently.

These differences can be summarized into three choices: siding with the British, siding with the Colonialists, or staying neutral. Whatever choice they made or did not make by staying neutral, they all had the same end result; each group lost lands to the Europeans. All groups were fighting for their freedom just like the Colonials. Despite this fact, once the Colonialists had won the war, even those who fought beside the Colonialists were not spared from their land grabbing.[92]

During the war, many Indians served as foot rangers. The origin of the ranger tradition lies in the seventeenth century wars between colonists and Native American tribes. In the original concept rangers were full-time soldiers employed by the colonial governments to "range" between fixed frontier fortifications as a reconnaissance system to provide early warning of hostile raids. In offensive operations they became scouts and guides, locating targets (such as villages) for task forces drawn from the militia or other colonial troops.

By 1676 a new element appeared in the ranger concept. Benjamin Church developed a special full-time unit mixing White colonists selected for frontier skills with friendly Indians to carry out offensive strikes against hostile Indians in terrain where normal militia units were ineffective. His memoirs published in 1716 are the first American military manual.[93]

One Indian company of foot rangers, under the supervision of Lt. John Withers, served with distinction in December of 1775. While Withers never stated that these Indians were Pee Dee, the fact that they were being used to quell slave revolts and that James Coachmen, with whom the Pee Dee had lived and assisted with other slave rebellions, strongly suggests Wither's company was comprised of Pee Dee Indians. That company was dismissed in December of 1775.[94] Another group of Pee Dee men who had lived on John Coachman's land were under the command of Colonel William Thompson. Many of these men received grants of land following the conclusion of the war.

Also in 1775, Captain John Allston, who had a plantation on the Pee Dee River,[95] acknowledged "full knowledge concerning the Pee Dee tribe of the Catawba confederacy."[96] In fact, Allston recruited from the Pee Dee Indians living near the Great Pee Dee River to form his company of "Foot Rovers," who were also called "Foot Rangers" or Raccoon Company," during the Revolutionary War.[97]

This company was composed entirely of Pee Dee Indians and was part of the regiment serving ... under Colonel William Thompson. The members of this company are some of the ancestors of current tribal members.

Of particular note is that Allston's company of Pee Dee Indians was comprised of members of both the Marlboro and Orangeburg County bands, many of whom were land owners in their respective areas. Clearly, contact and influence stretched across the miles and geography as late as the Revolutionary War, but this was to continue on only a very limited basis after the War. At that point, the two bands ceased to function as one large tribe and became instead a tribe divided, each with its autonomous government.

Allston's company was ultimately absorbed by Thompson's regiments the next year, with the majority ending up in his Third Regiment. Others went to either the Second or Fourth Regiments or into the companies of Captain Hopkins, Captain Felix Warley, Captain Joseph Warley or Captain Smith. William Bears, Robert Bird, John Bowen, John Bunch, Elisha, John, Phillip, and William 3Chavis, Moses Commins, James Carter, John Clark, John Cook, Daniel Gibson, Gilbert Grooms, John Hall, John Hunt, John, Joseph, Raymond, Richard and William Jones, Arnbrose Jackson, John and Calib Owens, John, James and Robert Reed, Joshua Reynolds, Cornelius Rose, James, John, George, and William Scott, James Sweat, Benjamin Thompson, Joab Wooton, and John, David and Joseph Williams served in Thompson's Third Regiment. John Chavis, James, Richard and William Clark, John Deas, David, Edward and Jacob George.

Silas Gibson, Joshue Hall, Burrell, James, Thomas, William and William T. Jones, William Lowrey and James Reed served in the Second Regiment, and John Hunt, John Jones and William Scott served under Captain Caldwell in the Fourth Regiment. John Bunch served under Captain Bunch, Thomas Oxendine under Captain Smith, and Levy Quick under Captain Joseph Warley. Elisha Chavers (Chavis), John, Robert and Thomas Gibson, and James Read served under Captain Felix Warley.

These particular men likely were placed under the supervision of Captain Felix Warley because James Coachman, with whom the Pee Dee helped quell a slave revolt, who gave the Pee Dee a place to stay in 1738 and who ultimately sold that land to the Manigault family to be used as their reservation, was the father of Benjamin Coachman, Warley's father-in-law.

Other Pee Dee served in mostly White units during the war. On May 20, 1776, Robert and Joseph Lockalier joined the army to fight for the Sixth Regiment. The war assisted the Pee Dee in getting back some of their land in the form of land grants for service in the war. Pee Dee Indians who received individual land grants continued farming their ancestral lands; all those who did not simply worked on larger White-owned farms or continued living in their beloved swamps.

Among those to receive grants because of military servers were those in the Chavis family, a name common among the Pee Dee. One John Chavis set up a trading post near the Four Holes end of the Edisto River; His brother Jordan Chavis lived on the Orangeburg end and served as a rafts man for trade goods.

In the Preliminary Articles of Peace of 1782, no mention was made of the Indians. Despite their important role and visible presence, they had receded into the shadows of European diplomacy. The Beaver Creek Pee Dee returned to their lands at the headwaters of the Edisto, and continued both farming and trading, activities that they had been involved in for centuries.

Among those to receive grants were those in the Chavis family, a name common among the Pee Dee. In 1784, members of that family were given land grants on both the Four Holes and Orangeburg County ends of the Edisto River.

One John Chavis set up a trading post near the Four Holes end of the Edisto River, while his brother, Jordan Chavis, lived on the Orangeburg end and served as a rafts man for trade goods. These Chavises are the descendants of the Pee Dee who had been living under a Pee Dee government among the Edisto of the Four Holes area, and are the ancestors of the Chavises and other Indians still living in the Orangeburg area.

The first Federal Census was taken in 1790, the majority of the last names found as "Free Persons Of Color," the designation often used for Indian people, were those who served in the Pee Dee company. Among the last names listed are Chavers (Chavis), Braveboy (Brayboy), Reed, Knight, Deas (also referred to on the census as Peedees), Scott, Swett, Hatcher and Jones.

In 1794, the South Carolina Legislature received a petition from Isaac Linagear, Isaac Mitchell, Jonathan Price, Spencer Bolton, William N. Sweat, and 29 other "free persons of color" seeking to repeal the "Act for imposing a poll tax on all free Negroes, mustees, and mulatoes." On April 6, 1832, a certificate was issued to South Carolina resident Sarah G. Jacobs, which cancelled her requirement to submit to the free Negro tax, included the fact that "she appears to be of Indian descent." A petition to the Legislature in 1859 inquiring if "persons of Indian descent are considered to be free persons of color and liable for the poll tax" caused a determination that Frederick Chavis, Lewis Chavis, Durany Chavis, James Jones, Mary Jones, and Jonathan Williams "do not qualify under the term 'free person of color' as they are of Indian ancestry."

In 1800, Pee Dee names found as "Free Persons of Color" on the Marlboro census include Chavis, Jones and Locklear. Those Pee Dee listed in the southern part of the Orangeburg district are Lovet Bunch, Elijah, Lazarus, Lettice Chavers (Chavis), Shadrak, Willis, Charity, Cloe and Hardy Read, John Reynolds, Peter and John Rouse, Abraham and William Scott, Swett, Isaac Jones and Abraham and Amy Williams.

Also listed are additional names associated with the Pee Dee and other Indian communities: Lewis Braveboy, Phillip Bonner, Cary Collins, John Chandler, John Fitts, James Newness, Tamer Nagin and George Galphin (the half-Indian son of Indian trader George Galphin, with whom the Beaver Creek Pee Dee worked).

In all, approximately 133 of the Beaver Creek Pee Dee, were living near the swamps of the Edisto River in the Orangeburg District. A decade later, in 1800, Pee Dee names found as "Free Persons of Color" such as Chavis and Jones are still found in Orangeburg County.

Persons living in 1808 remembered at least 30 Pee Dee Indians living in the St. Stephens and St. John's area. King John was chief of this remnant. By 1808, there was reportedly only one half-breed woman left in that area.[98] Many had moved to the North-Neeses-Salley area in Orangeburg County to join with the Beaver Creek Pee Dee, others returned to the Marlboro/Dillon County areas as well.

The oral stories passed down by the Elders of the Pee Dee Indians tells a very different version of what happened to the Pee Dee people than what has been written about them. Between 1730 and 1800 all of the smaller tribes such as the Pee Dee were almost destroyed by disease, attacks by both larger tribes and the White farmers that wanted their small farming areas near the rivers. The Pee Dee Indians had no defense of the law because South Carolina had already changed their status of being Indian to Mulatto, Croatan, and Free person of color. The few Pee Dee Indians and other small tribes were forced to become part of the White man's world.

From the early 1800's until the Civil War of 1861-1865 the descendants of the Original Pee Dee Indians had become small family clans that lived on the rivers and also some were sharecroppers for the White farmers that were the descendants of the settlers that were helped by the Pee Dee Indians to defeat the Red Coats and a host of other Indian tribes all the way down to Florida. The Pee Dee Indians fought in the Civil War and there are many tribal members that trace their Indian Heritage back to those Soldiers.

From the late 1790's thru the Indian removal acts of the 1830's the Pee Dee Indians and other small Bands and Clans were partially assimilated into the White man's way of life, they abandoned the round type of dwelling and built log cabins on the land that was available to them. By the start of the Civil War in 1861 the Pee Dees that had escaped the removal of Indians to the West had become sharecroppers and Farm workers and lived in small family clans along the Pee Dee Rivers.

After the Civil War the Pee Dee Indians were not recognized as Indians by the census takers. The trend of not identifying Indians as Indians continued as before the war. No real logical reason can be identified as to why South Carolina did not identify and accept Indians as Indians. The Pee Dee Indians believe it was done due to the fact that after the removal of the "Cherokee Indians " Known as the Trail of Tears, South Carolina assumed that there were no Indians left in South Carolina and to make this a true fact any person that did not have White skin was considered to be of mixed blood, which could be Black and White or Black and Indian - anyone with dark skin was a Mulatto, Croatan, or Black. Anyone not of pure White blood was subject to the rigorous apartheid system of the South.

Chapter 7: The Aftermath of the Fight for Freedom

For a decade after the war, life went relatively unchanged for the Pee Dee. Then a group of Pee Dee Indians living just across the Orangeburg County line in Edgefield County petitioned to have their children admitted to the schools that were established in that area for free persons. Their children had not been admitted to Free School No.3 because only White children were allowed in those schools. Those listed on the petition, who were living on Chavers Creek, were James Reynolds, Adam Carpenter, John Wootan, Lewis S. John (son of Chief Lewis Jones), Richard Solley, Matthew Hamilton, Winfrey Whitlock, William Smith, Thomas Maybury, and M.F. Johnson.

During this time period, members of the tribe who owned land tried to hold onto it, often unsuccessfully, and those who sold their land, like Jordan Chavis,[99] who in 1814 sold eight tracts of land mostly to the Quick family, tried to follow tribal tradition of keeping the land within the tribe. Others simply continued to work the fields of others and to fish and hunt in the old ways to support their families.

As settlers pressed against western lands controlled by Native Americans, violence repeatedly erupted between them. Andrew Jackson came to the office of President determined to pave the way for American settlers. In 1830 he signed the Indian Removal Act, which allowed him to offer Native Americans land in unsettled areas west of the Mississippi, in exchange for their lands in existing states. They had no say to change this. They protested and went to courts, but they had no power in U.S. government and their personal votes did not count. The courts ruled against them although Chief Justice John Marshall declared, "...that an Indian tribe or nation within the United States is not a foreign state in the sense of the constitution...". They were considered a part of the United States, yet no democracy existed for the Native Americans. Their reasoning and advocated desires were ignored. The Indian Removal Act of 1830 ordered soldiers to imprison Native Americans in stockades.

Stealing lands from Native Americans and being dishonest with treaties was a violation of their legal rights. Our people had been living on that land for years--way before the U.S. even existed! We helped White Americans and established formal treaties with the U.S. that guaranteed our residence, privileges, and peace from intruders. However, a letter from Cherokee Chief John Ross says otherwise...In his letter, Ross protests to the Senate and House of Representatives of how trespassers have looted, hurt, and even killed members of his tribe. Despite the treaties and the laws enforcing them, Native Americans were still being disturbed, and although, the treaties were still active during the Removal Act; their lands were taken.

The human rights of Native Americans were violated. They were not treated as human beings and their cause considered subordinate to the United States by Andrew Jackson in his defense of the Removal Policy in 1830. Jackson referred to them as 'savages' and they were treated much like livestock as the Removal Policy took place. A private sent to carry out the Removal Policy by the name of John G. Bernett, describes how Native Americans were herded like cattle to the west. Their basic human rights were not just violated; they were exterminated. While some tribes accepted this solution, others, including the Pee Dee resisted, retreating to the more undesirable areas such as the mountains of western Carolinas and the borderland areas of the Pee Dee River basin.[100]

Many members of the tribe began assimilation into White society, helping to avoid removal to present-day Oklahoma in the early 19th Century. The legacy of this assimilation led to a number of issues in the 20th Century. During segregation, it was seen as advantageous to identify as "White." Since many Pee Dee were already of mixed ancestry, people began to pass in order to make their day to day lives easier. Those whose complexions were darker were often forced to go to "Black" schools. However, there were a few Indian schools around the Neeses, South Carolina and Charleston, South Carolina areas during that time. Some other Pee Dee establishments were also created and continue to be maintained to this day. One of these is the Rocky Swamp Methodist Church. Currently, a combination of Methodist and Native American Church religions is observed there. Many Pee Dee people are buried in its historic cemetery.

The Federal Census of 1850 shows that several of the Pee Dee surnames were by that time found among the Lumbee in Robeson County, many of those listed on the 1850 census with last names such as Locklear, Chavis, Lowrie, Brigman, Evans, Roberts and Hall, are listed as having been born either in South Carolina or in Scotland or Richmond Counties, North Carolina. Several other people with Pee Dee surnames, such as Hunt, Quick and Brayboy (Braveboy), are listed as having been born in Robeson County. These are possibly the descendants of the Pee Dee who went to that area 100 years earlier (1850 Federal Census of Robeson County, N.C.) or of intermarriage between the two distinct tribes.

At a time when fear of removal from tribal homelands permeated Native American communities, many native people served in the military during the Civil War. These courageous men fought with distinction, knowing they might jeopardize their freedom, unique cultures, and ancestral lands if they ended up on the losing side of the White man's war.

In an interesting twist of history, General Ely S. Parker, a member of the Seneca tribe, drew up the articles of surrender which General Robert E. Lee signed at Appomattox Court House on April 9, 1865. Gen. Parker, who served as Gen. Ulysses S. Grant's military secretary and was a trained attorney, was once rejected for Union military service because of his race. At Appomattox, Lee is said to have remarked to Parker, "I am glad to see one real American here," to which Parker replied, "We are all Americans."

Approximately 20,000 Native Americans served in the Union and Confederate armies during the Civil War, participating in battles such as Pea Ridge, Second Manassas, Antietam, Spotsylvania, Cold Harbor, and in Federal assaults on Petersburg. By fighting with the White man, Native Americans hoped to gain favor with the prevailing government by supporting the war effort. They also saw war service as a means to end discrimination and relocation from ancestral lands to western territories. Instead, the Civil War proved to be the Native American's last effort to stop the tidal wave of American expansion.

In the east, many tribes that had yet to suffer removal took sides in the Civil War. The Thomas Legion, an Eastern Band of Confederate Cherokee, led by Col. William Holland Thomas, fought in the mountains of Tennessee and North Carolina. Another 200 Cherokee formed the Junaluska Zouaves. Nearly all Catawba adult males served the South in the 5th, 12th and 17th South Carolina Volunteer Infantry, or the Army of Northern Virginia. They distinguished themselves in the Peninsula Campaign, at Second Manassas, and Antietam, and in the trenches at Petersburg. A monument in Columbia, South Carolina, honors the Catawba's service in the Civil War. As a consequence of the regiments' high rate of dead and wounded, the continued existence of the Catawba people was jeopardized.[101]

During the Civil War from 1861-1865, both bands of Pee Dee Indians continued their historic allegiance to the South Carolina government by supporting the Confederacy. Many members of the tribe, including Francis and William Hall, served in the Confederate Army. Francis Hall even served for a time at Fort Sumter, although he and his brother suffered periodic self-inflicted injuries which allowed them to return home to their family.

A number of the Pee Dee from Orangeburg served during the war and appeared on the pension lists published in the Orangeburg Times and Democrat. On August 25, 1897, that newspaper reported that the following people could get their pension money from Clerk of Court G. L. Salley: Class C, No. 2 – Josiah Chavis, Phillip Chavis, Calvin Chavis and William Chavis; Class No.4 - Rachel Chavis. On May 29, 1901, an additional list was published: Class C, No.1 - J. C. Chavis; Class C., No.2 - W.C. Chavis, Pickens Chavis and William Chavis. A final list was published in the Times and Democrat on April 27, 1904: Class C No 2 - John A. Chavis, W .L. Chavis, J. C. Chavis, Pickens Chavis, and W.C. Chavis, All of these people were living in the area where the Beaver Creek Pee Dee moved in the 1750's, the area where they continue to live today.

The Marlboro County list of those serving in Company D of the 26th S.C. Infantry included a number of Chavises as well. Alex Chavis, Alfred Chavis, C.J. "Calvin" Chavis, Eli Chavis, Eliab Chavis, Harris Chavis, James Chavis, Nelson Chavis, Noah Chavis, W. Chavis and W .J .Chavis served in that company. Of those, C.J. and Eliab were both held as prisoners of war at Lookout Point, Maryland from March or April of 1865 to June 26, 1865, when they were released. Eliab is listed on prison records as having a dark complexion and Black hair, with dark hazel eyes. C.J. is reported to have Dark hair and grey eyes. Alfred and Nelson Chavis were killed.

Also serving were George, John and W. Chavis, all born in Marlboro County. These men served in Company B of the 24th S.C. Infantry. George died during the war. In 1901, Alex, Murray and Willis J. Chavis were on the Confederate Pension List, as were widows Mary and Mary Anna Chavis. In 1902, Perry Chavis was also on that list. A large number of Chavises from the Orangeburg settlement served in the war as well.

While the war raged and African Americans were proclaimed free, the U.S. government continued its policies of pacification and removal of Native Americans. Despite any Federal government proclamations, the South retained an apartheid system that identified people as white, mixed blood, or black.

Chapter 8: The Pee Dee and Share Cropping

The South's loss in the Civil War represented the first time the Pee Dee had been on the losing side of a conflict. Unlike their Lumbee neighbors to the north, neither band of Pee Dee had sided with the Union. Yet while the South may have been defeated in the Civil War, the people who returned to their farms were the same people who had been there prior to the war .The Pee Dee's neighbors had not changed.

Before the Civil War, slaves and indentured servants were considered personal property, and they or their descendants could be sold or inherited like any other property. Like other property, human chattel was governed largely by laws of individual states. Generally, these laws concerning indentured servants and slaves did not differentiate between the sexes. Some, however, addressed only women. Regardless of their country of origin, many early immigrants were indentured servants, people who sold their labor in exchange for passage to the New World and housing on their arrival. Initially, most laws passed concerned indentured servants, but around the middle of the seventeenth century, colonial laws began to reflect differences between indentured servants and slaves. More important, the laws began to differentiate between races: the association of "servitude for natural life" with people of African descent became common. *Re Negro John Punch* (1640) was one of the early cases that made a racial distinction among indentured servants.[102]

After the slave trade officially ended, many slave owners tried to ensure that sufficient numbers of slaves were available to work their plantations. Slave women of childbearing age became more valuable. There are a number of court cases concerning slave women who either killed their masters who forced them to have sexual relations or killed the children rather than have the children enslaved.[103]

Miscegenation laws, forbidding marriage between races, were prevalent in the South and the West. Because English masters had had little regard for indentured servants of non-Anglo ethnic groups, they allowed and sometimes encouraged commingling of their servants. Being seen in public or bringing legitimacy to these relations, however, was not lawful. This is evinced by a court decision from 1630, the first court decision in which a Negro woman and a white man figured prominently. *Re Davis* (1630) concerned sexual relations between them, the decision stating, "Hugh Davis to be soundly whipt . . . for abusing himself to the dishonor of God and shame of Christianity by defiling his body in lying with a Negro, which fault he is to acknowledge next Sabbath day."[104]

Following the American Revolution, members of the tribe had began assimilation into White society, helping to avoid the impact of such laws. Later they had to fear removal to present-day Oklahoma in the early 19th Century under President Andrew Jackson regime. The legacy of this assimilation led to a number of issues in the 20th Century. During segregation, it was seen as advantageous to identify as "White." Since many Pee Dee were already of mixed ancestry, people began to pass in order to make their day to day lives easier. Those whose complexions were darker were often forced to go to "Black" schools. However, there were a few Indian schools in South Carolina during that time. Some other Pee Dee establishments were also created and continue to be maintained to this day. One of these is the Rocky Swamp Methodist Church. Currently, a combination of Methodist and Native American Church religions is observed there. Many Pee Dee people are buried in its historic cemetery

So while the next years were difficult for the tribe, members of the Pee Dee struggled alongside their White neighbors just to get by and feed their families while members of the Lumbee were at odds with their neighbors. At the same time, with Indian troubles brewing in the west, the Pee Dee opted again for peaceable co-existence. Members of the tribe kept quiet about their identities, and began forming their own governments in ways less obvious to their neighbors.

Despite these attempts at concealment, trouble came to the Pee Dee as farmers tried to replace slave labor as cheaply as possible. During the early years of the Civil War, Native Americans had tended their crops and tried to retain their tenuous hold on land. As the war progressed and the Confederacy began to experience increasing labor shortages, the Confederacy began to conscript labor.

As disenfranchised persons unable to vote or bear arms, Native Americans were easy prey. They were forced into the labor camps of a Confederacy to whom they felt no allegiance or sympathy. Many were shot for attempting to evade conscription. Still others succumbed to starvation, disease and despair.

The end of the Civil War did not end the suffering of Native Americans. White Americans continued to desire Native American lands, and resorted to "tied mule" incidents in order to get free Native American labor and title to Native American land. Although the possession of property by free persons of color did not come under direct legislative assault; the "tied mule" stories illustrate one form of a more general process of land loss suffered by disfranchised. A White farmer had only to find his mule tied up on a neighboring Native American's land to file a complaint for theft with the local authorities.

The Native American farmer was promptly arrested for theft. "Tied mule" incidents were resolved with the Native American paying a fine, or giving up a portion of his land, or agreeing to work for the "wronged" White farmer for free. Those who did not agree were often found hanging from a convenient tree.[105] This was all a part of share-cropping.

During Reconstruction, Indians, former slaves, and many small White farmers became trapped in this new system of economic exploitation. Lacking capital and land of their own, they were forced to work for large landowners. Initially, planters, with the support of the Freedmen's Bureau, sought to restore gang labor under the supervision of White overseers. Those who wanted autonomy and independence, refused to sign contracts that required gang labor. Ultimately, sharecropping emerged as a sort of compromise.

With defeat came emancipation for nearly 60 percent of South Carolinians, and White and Black Carolinians were forced to work out a new relationship. In late 1865, White Carolinians took advantage of lenient federal policies to create a new state government filled with former

Confederates, who imposed restrictive Black codes that circumscribed Black civil rights and later rejected the Fourteenth Amendment.[106]

In response, Congress ordered military rule and a new state government. In 1868, a constitutional convention that welcomed freedmen created a new government recognizing Black voting rights, removing property qualifications for office holding, and creating a free public school system.

Until 1876, the Republican Party controlled state government, and African Americans held office at every level but governor, achieving a greater degree of political power in South Carolina than in any other state. South Carolina's Whites reacted violently to this turn of events.

A reign of terror by the Ku Klux Klan during 1870 and 1871 resulted in so many lynching and beatings of Republicans that the writ of habeas corpus was suspended in nine upstate counties. However, in the aftermath the federal government failed to make more than a token show of force and terror organizations continued to function in South Carolina.

In the disputed election of 1876, the Red Shirts, a White paramilitary organization, managed to engineer an apparent Democratic victory through violence and fraud. The Compromise of 1877 ended federal support for Republican Party government in South Carolina, and the White minority, represented by the Democratic Party and led by former Confederate General Wade Hampton III, regained control of state government.

Instead of cultivating land in gangs supervised by overseers, landowners divided plantations into 20 to 50 acre plots suitable for farming by a single family. In exchange for land, a cabin, and supplies, sharecroppers agreed to raise a cash crop (usually cotton).

They also agreed to give half the crop to their landlord. The high interest rates landlords and sharecroppers charged for goods bought on credit (sometimes as high as 70 percent a year) transformed sharecropping into a system of economic dependency and poverty. The freedmen found that "freedom could make folks proud but it didn't make 'em rich."[107]

As Hampton and the old elite (the so-called "Bourbons") returned to power, they tried to recreate the world of antebellum South Carolina. However, their inattention to the state's agricultural problems and mildly tolerant racial policies soon led to political revolt. Benjamin R. Tillman rode the disaffection of the state's White farmers to the governor's office, where he and his allies attacked the symbols of Bourbon power, if not the substance.

Tillman focused his "reform" impulse on removing the state's Black majority from public life. His triumph was the state's Constitution of 1895, which disfranchised the Black majority and laid the groundwork for White supremacy and one-party Democratic rule in the twentieth century. In the last years of the nineteenth century and early years of the twentieth, South Carolina's White government also enacted a host of laws designed to segregate public life. Relations between the races not governed by law were controlled by rigid customs that ensured Blacks and Indians inferior status. As a result, Black Carolinians left the state in droves, most bound for northern cities. After about 1922, South Carolina no longer had a Black majority.

The economy remained overwhelmingly agricultural and the system of sharecropping and farm tenancy led to heavy dependence on cotton, whose prices were in decline because of overproduction. As a result, farmers in the state's northeastern Pee Dee region turned increasingly to tobacco cultivation, which soon witnessed its own cycle of overproduction and declining prices.

In the last years of the nineteenth and the early decades of the twentieth century, South Carolinians began to diversify their economy, primarily into extractive industries such as cotton textiles. Textile mills were organized across the Piedmont region, taking advantage of waterpower and a surplus of White labor, but creating new class tensions in the process.

While some in the nation tried to help newly freed African-American slaves, the general prejudice against Indians did not moderate. The South continued its practice of apartheid. In response, members of the tribe kept quiet about their identity and began conducting their own government business in ways less obvious to their neighbors.

Chapter 9: The Churches and the Pee Dee

Until the early 19th century, the boundary line between North and South Carolina was still under dispute and the area was generally considered "ungoverned." The Presbyterian Church, founded in America in 1706, largely restricted their ministerial attentions to the growing Scotch-Irish settlements, an ethnic group which had a strong history of involvement in the Presbyterian Church in Britain and in allegiance to Calvinist doctrine, both in Europe and America. The proselytizing activities of Baptists and Methodists, however, were concerted and far-reaching, and were perceived by the Anglican establishment as representing a considerable threat to the established Southern social and political order.

Anglicans were forbearing on the issue of slavery. Indeed, many Anglicans were slave owners. Baptists and Methodists, avowedly condemnatory on the issue and practice of slavery, threatened the hierarchy of class that bounded the free and un-free - freedom being defined by ownership of property and/or people, and the state of being owned.

George Whitfield and John Wesley were the first Methodists to preach the gospel along the southeastern frontier. James Oglethorpe, Georgia's colonial governor, warned Wesley to stay away from the Choctaw for fear of retaliation from the Catholic French. Taking Oglethorpe's advice, Wesley confined his ministry to the Savannah and Charleston areas. However, after only two years, Wesley returned to England in 1739, having considered his Methodist mission among the Indians a failure.

Records of missionary activity in the southeast are scanty at best. When the Methodist Episcopal Church was founded in Baltimore in 1784, there seems to have been no concerted attempt by Methodists themselves to reap a rich harvest of souls among the unconverted.

The general lack of evidence for missionary activity suggests that Indians were already practicing some form of Christianity by the time of the most widespread Baptist and Methodist proselytizing during the 18th and 19th centuries. Christian communities for Baptists and Methodists alike were modeled on the primitive Christian communities depicted in the New Testament.

The Christian tenets propounded by these evangelical missionaries of economic and spiritual equality, godly discipline and self-abasement were sure to appeal to a class of people with limited access to surplus and wealth. By 1790, about 14 percent of White southerners and 4 percent of Blacks were members of Baptist or Methodist churches.

It must be noted prior to this time; Indians had suffered greatly from the encroachment of Europeans. Wide-spread disease had wiped out the majority of Indians in the Southeast. This combined with economic problems and military defeats left most Indians questioning their own traditions. Their survival seemed linked to the Europeans.

Settlement Indians had to adapt to European ways in order to survive. This led to division within tribes as some members tried to maintain traditions. The colonists exploited this division to pit Indian against Indian in local disputes. Yet, even those Indians who accepted Christianity subtlety resisted outright amalgamation by organizing their own churches and hybridizing their practices. Some tribes even developed their own Messianic religions.

By providing a sense of community, the churches aided the survival of Indians in the Southeast. They allow disparate groups of Indians to come together and support each other, ignoring earlier conflicts.

That some Indians were already familiar with the tenets of Christianity is evidenced by a hymn written before 1776 by a Native American woman.

De joy I felt I cannot tell
To tink dat I was saved from Hell
Through Jesus streaming blood
Dat I am saved by grace divine

Who am de wurst of all mankind
O glory be to God.
So me lub God wid inside heart
He fight for me, he take um part.

He save um life before
God hear poor Indian in de wood.
So me lub him and dat be good.
Me prize him evermore.

Not much is known about the establishment of churches among the Indians of Dillon County. By the 19th century however, Baptist and Methodist missionaries were busy in South Carolina. Many more churches of various denominations would follow, with many new churches still being founded.

One can speculate that the creation of Indian churches had as much to do with "outside" defined classifications of Indian socio-political status in a highly racial South, as well as an inclusionary concern for the spiritual well-being and sustenance of the Indian community. Before the Civil War, churches, meeting houses, and preaching places were tri-racial. Legally, there was nothing to prevent members of any of the diverse ethnic communities of the south from sitting together at worship.

The Civil War era proved to be a turning point for Indian people socially and spiritually. Indian churches for Indian people emerged as well as Indian schools for Indian students. Brush harbor gatherings gave rise to worshipping congregations meeting regularly and our first Baptist churches came into existence. Indian preachers were in short supply but many good-hearted White preachers reached out to preach the gospel wherever it would be received by Indians.

By Reconstruction, a great change took place within the Robeson Circuit. In 1870, non-White members were "separated out" from the rolls of these meeting houses and told to fend for themselves. The Methodist Episcopal Church, South, decreed that its membership was to be exclusively White. Due to this exclusion, Indians founded and directed our own churches.

Rejected by White churches but not entirely by the White missionary preachers, Indians continued the worship of God and accepting the Christian faith in indigenous churches. At the time Indian communities began providing for their own Christian spiritual needs, they also assumed responsibility for educating their own Native people. No state assistance for public education was available for Carolina Indian communities.

Of particular note to the Indian people were the 1850s-1870s suppression of and the 1880s criminalization of "Indian religion." It is doubtless no coincidence that the Pee Dee during this time period suddenly began forming their churches. The tribe saw these formations as a way to continue self-governance without the influence of their non-Indian neighbors.

Churches weren't the only means of government used by the Pee Dee during this period. In the late 1800's, according to tribal elder Lettie "Aunt Miss" Locklear , a Pee Dee Indian at Willow Pond served as a type of magistrate to mediate disputes among tribal members.

However, as the tribe began to grow once again, more churches were needed, and in 1891, Pee Dee Freewill Baptist Church was "organized by the Indians near Parishes Mill in upper Dillon County.[108] The Pee Dee Chapel Baptist Church was formally organized in 1896 after meeting for years in rural brush arbors.[109] Neil Chavis was one of the two people who received lumber from the Edwin McInnis to build that Church. Neil received the land because the Indians were seeking to have a place of worship of their own. Neil was not only Native he was thought of as a leader and was influential in the area at that time.

Additionally, since he built the church, that was attended by Indians and set aside from the local White and Black Churches, provides strong proof that Neil was a Pee Dee and a leader in the Pee Dee Community. Locally, the church was well known as an Indian church. The name was later changed to Pee Dee Missionary Baptist Church, and the congregation replaced its original building in 1952. Among its Indian pastors was Grady Hunt. The original deed was issued the trustees of the chapel.

John Dallas Locklear born in1886 married Lizzie Chavis in 1909. The marriage produced eleven children. He attended Pee Dee Baptist Church for many years. After leaving Pee Dee Baptist Church, he purchased land for $50 from Hector McRae on which he built and was the founder of Leland Grove Baptist Church in 1923.

A school building was purchased for $250 and moved for use as the first church building. In 1969, the present church was built with donations from the congregation and from English Jones, the Dean of Pembroke State College, and from L.S. McColl. Among the elders that governed the Leland Grove Baptist Church were Lizzie Chavis Locklear (1896 – 1981), O.T Moore (1908 – 2002), Macey Locklear Barfield (1916 -) and Belulah C. Bethea (1908 – 1992.

Chapter 10: Pee Dee and the Schools

Except for their names on Federal censuses and occasional affidavits attesting to their race, we know relatively little about Indian Communities in the low country until the late 19th century, when several factors will converge to shed additional light on them. An increase in both population and deeded land began to concentrate the Indian population in more defined communities.

Those communities begin to create an institutional life that gave form and definition to them in the historical record. They also came to the attention of educational reformers who promoted universal schooling. And finally, South Carolina began to enact segregation laws that formalized race relations and drew the color line rather rigidly between Black and White, leaving no place for Indians.

Indian children could not attend White schools, and, by choice, did not attend the Black schools either. A few small elementary schools for Indians were finally approved in various communities. In later years, changes in Public Laws allowed for such schools among Indians in other eastern counties. However, there were no opportunities for natives beyond elementary grades to gain education diplomas or degrees.

In 1878, the Pee Dee of McColl followed the lead of their Orangeburg cousins with the founding of the Leland Grove Pee Dee Chapel in Dillon County formally organized in 1896 after meeting for years in rural brush arbors.[110] This was also the site of the Leland Grove Indian School in the early 20th century. Also known as the Brayboy School, it was the center of education for Indian children starting in the 1920s.[111] The school taught 1st through 7th grade Indian children.

Principal James Brayboy took over the school in 1947 and ran it until it closed in 1970. Mr. Brayboy is still remembered in Dillon County. Most of his students ended their educations when they graduated from the 7th grade rather than trying to integrate into the other Dillon County schools.[112]

In 1896, the South Carolina Legislature recognized the "Croatan Indians" within the state. These "Croatans" were really the Pee Dee Indians. Four years later, in 1900, Leland Grove Freewill Baptist Church was organized near the Dillon County town of Little Rock near McInnis's bridge. The church was constructed from the old Carolina School Building and was by 1928 to be the home of the Leland Grove Indian School.[113]

As the 20th century began, the series of laws known as Jim Crow laws came into existence. The passing of these laws reinforced the Pee Dees perception that it was important to be quiet about being Indian.[114]

In 1910, Dillon County had its first census as a county in its own right, having been formed that year from Marion County. That year marked the area's first and only "Special Indian Census." Neither the Marlboro County nor the Orangeburg County censuses contained similar "Indian censuses" despite the fact that the Indians of both of those counties were the cousins of those on the Dillon Census. Seventy-three individuals residing in the Hamer Community were identified as Indian on that census. These were the same people who on previous and subsequent censuses who were more often listed as mulatto or White.

It was in this way that the state had attempted to deny the racial identity of its Indian people. Ten years earlier, in 1900, Scotland County, N.C, had conducted a "Special Indian Census" of its own. The majority of the current members of the Marlboro/Dillon County Pee Dee have at least one and usually several ancestors listed on one or both of these two censuses.

The fact that the state was suddenly willing to acknowledge any of the Pee Dee were Indian is remarkable, considering they had been consistently misidentified since the very first censuses. Both the Pee Dee and their relations in Marlboro and Dillon Counties had typically been listed on censuses as mulatto, with occasional listings as Black and White, despite widespread community knowledge that these were Indian people and documentation, such as affidavits of Indian ancestry, confirming that fact. This trend continued when the state of South Carolina began keeping records of deaths in 1915.

The misidentification of the Pee Dee's racial heritage on the death certificates was not complete. From the very beginning, some of the members of the both bands of Pee Dee were recognized as "Croatan" or "Indian." These identities seemed to materialize from nowhere, as the state would list parents and family members of the deceased on census records as anything but Indian, making them Black, White or mulatto instead. James Clark, of Marlboro County, died July 15, 1915, was listed as a Croatan Indian on his death certificate. No parents were listed, and

Clark was buried in Locklear Cemetery. (S.C. Death Certificate #14341) On Sept. 10, 1916, a Chavis infant, the son of Aaron Chavis and Maggie Hut to Chavis of Orangeburg County was listed as a "Croatan Indian," as was Julia Jackson, the daughter of Eliza Mims, who died June 18, 1918. Blanche Martin, a daughter of Lewis Scott and Mary Bunch, died Dec. 14, 1935 and was listed as "Croatan Indian," as was George Williams, a son of Samuel Williams and Ollie Hoover Williams who died July 13, 1916, and Leon Earnest Williams, son of Emma Williams who died July 28, 1915. All of these people were born in Orangeburg County. Family members of these people were often listed as some other race, depending largely on their skin tone and the perceptions or prejudices of the person filling out the death certificate.

Still, experts on the Indians of the area knew even at that time that the Pee Dee people had maintained their Indian identity, culture and history. In 1908, Chapman Milling, author of <u>Red Carolinians,</u> a definitive work on the Indians of South Carolina, wrote a letter to Dr. Frank Speck regarding the Pee Dee. Speck, a linguist who is noted for his work on the

Catawba language and for his book <u>Catawba Texts,</u> had inquired whether the Indians of Darlington County knew anything of their history. Milling said that the half-bloods living in Darlington County had been slaves and did not know their history. He suggested he talk to the Pee Dee instead, who he said "have lived in the same place for generations and I think in all probability you might get information concerning their former history from them."

School soon became another place for the tribe to nurture and sustain itself. By the 1920's, South Carolina maintained three separate school systems, one each for Whites, Blacks and Indians. So in 1928, Leland Grove Indian School was founded at Leland Grove Freewill Baptist Church. The school served only Indian children from the Pee Dee community.

Four Pine School served the Indian children of Neeses then, in Orangeburg County, and Sardis Indian School also served the Indian children of Dillon County. Sardis Indian School was not open for many years, but Leland Grove remained open until 1970. When the Indian schools were later closed, the state attempted to send many of the children to Black schools. Light-skinned children, however, were allowed to attend White schools.

In 1930, the Dillon census claimed 365 Indian inhabitants. In 1938, yet another Indian church, Fairview Methodist Church, was founded. By this time, the sheer number of churches and schools serving primarily Indian people forces a serious question of this number. In fact, other records make it clear that misidentification of the Pee Dee Indians was still occurring.

For example, in 1941, a Locklear infant from Clio in Marlboro County is listed as Indian on her death certificate. (S.C. Death Certificate) Her father, Evans Locklear, was listed on some censuses as mulatto and others as White.

Chapter 11: The Pee Dee Emerge from the Shadows

Things continued relatively quietly for the Pee Dee for the next three decades, with tribal government continuing through the churches and schools and what tribal heritage there was left being taught through the families. Then, in 1970, Leland Grove Indian School finally closed its doors. Indian children were sent to other schools within the South Carolina school system. That year, the Federal census listed 2,241 Indians living in South Carolina. Many of these were living in Marlboro and Dillon Counties.

The closure of the school left a large hole for the Pee Dee people in Marlboro and Dillon Counties that they are quick to relate to this day. Many Pee Dee had attended the 8 years at Leland Grove only to drop out rather than attend a Black or White secondary school. Many members have personal stories of the discrimination faced by Indians at non-Indian schools. The result is an illiteracy rate of over 35% within the tribe.

In November, 1976, the Pee Dee finally brought their tribal government back into the open. Bernice Hunt, Charles Jacobs, Willie Goins, Elizabeth Perrit, Dorine Locklear and Homer Campbell, in the hopes of following tribal tradition of the tribe being responsible for caring for and governing itself, incorporated under the name of the Pee Dee Indian Association. They were content, for the time, to govern their own affairs through their churches and families. It would take 22 more years for their Beaver Creek cousins to follow suit.

It was clear their work was cut out for them. In the years of functioning within the churches and the parameters of the federal government, the Pee Dee Indians had suffered. In 1979, newspaper reports said twenty percent of Indians in Marlboro County lived below poverty line. Tribal leaders knew the number was significantly higher.

In 1980, Representative Parker Evatt, R-Richland, proposed state recognition for the Pee Dee, Santee and Edisto Indian peoples. The bill did not pass. That year, however, the Pee Dee Adult Education Center was opened to teach reading, spelling, and math. The next October, the Administration for Native Americans, gave the Pee Dee a grant for $52,050 for the "basic needs of Indian people."

For the next several years, the tribe worked to increase the public's awareness of the Pee Dee people. On March 18, 1982, the tribe sent delegates to the Indian Unity Conference. On Nov. 11 of that year, the Pee Dee celebrated Indian Week. In October of 1983, Gary Wallen was elected sub-chief of the tribe. He presented an Indian Awareness program at the Adamsville School. That year, Dorine Locklear becomes only female Indian Chief in state of South Carolina, continuing the tribe's still-held matriarchal tradition. In 1984, Karen Montoya, Chief David Locklear and Carmela Kitchin were honored by JTPA. On March 28 of that year, a tornado devastated Indian community, killing several and leaving others homeless.

A September 2, 1985 newspaper article said Marlboro County led state in Indian voters, with 119. Richland County had 80, and Dillon County had 78. That was also the year Gene Crediford began work on his "Those Who Remain" photo exhibit of the state's Indian people, including the Pee Dee.

It wasn't until 1986, 216 years after the colonists arrived that the Pee Dee finally got a taste of state recognition. That year, Governor Richard "Dick" Riley formed the Palmetto Indian Affairs Commission, effectively giving state recognition to the Pee Dee, Catawba, Santee and Edisto Indian tribes. Their second Pow-wow, held October of that year, was indeed cause to celebrate. Republican Governor Carroll Campbell later refused to acknowledge Riley's executive order.

In May of 1987, the South Carolina House and Senate passed a bill supporting the tribe, as well as the Santee and the Edisto, and recommending the tribes be granted Federal Recognition by the Bureau of Indian Affairs.

However, this historic bill did not mark the end of the Pee Dee's quest for recognition, as the state soon began to behave as if the bill had never existed.

During this time, the tribe also worked to keep tribal traditions alive. In April of 1987, the Pee Dee organized more job training programs. Rodney Roller was named chief, just in time for the August 8 Pow-Wow, the Pee Dee's third. In October of that year, Karen Montoya organized the Wind Walkers Indian Dance Team to teach the Pee Dee children traditional songs and dance. In 1988, Senator John Lindsay visited the Pee Dee at a tea held in his honor by the Pee Dee Indians.

Additionally, the tribe worked to assist others in need. In 1989, Pee Dee members helped migrants in Paxville who were victims of Hurricane Hugo. Still, they had to work to help their own as well. That year, newspaper reports state that thirty-four percent of Indians in Marlboro County were living below poverty line.

The 1990 Federal census listed 426 Indians living in Dillon County, and 85 living in Marion County .More than 2,500 were listed on the tribal roll at that time, so tribal members believe the census significantly undercounted the number of Indians in the area.

One year later, in 1991, Pee Dee tribe negotiated to open the Pee Dee Indian School of International Trade in the old abandoned Adamsville Middle School. Although the tribe was at first given the building, the negotiation fell through less than three months later and the project is abandoned. The project was one of many attempts by the tribe to achieve self-sufficiency.

Chiefs of all four Pee Dee tribes in South Carolina came together in 1992 to denounce the Council of Native Americans of South Carolina. On Sept. 16 of that year, the Pee Dee helped the Miccosukee Indian Tribe after Hurricane Andrew. In 1996, the Pee Dee Indian Association, in the spirit of cooperation with the state of South Carolina, petitioned for legislative acknowledgment of its state recognition. The bill passed the House with ease but was killed by the Senate majority leader at the request of Governor David Beasley.

The move by no means disheartened the tribe. By this point, members of the tribe were working together to file a petition for federal recognition. A grant from the Methodist Church's Blaine Trust gave the tribe the capacity to open a computer center for its youth. At the same time, the tribe was allowed to lease land from the county and a private family in order to set up a produce stand and with the hopes of establishing a farm to provide jobs and income for its people.

The Pee Dee also participated in a Unity Conference organized to unite all of the state's tribes and urban Indian organizations. That Conference led the way for efforts to reinstate the Palmetto Indian Affairs Commission. The efforts proved successful, and in February of 1997, Governor David Beasley agreed to sign into existence the South Carolina Indian Affairs Commission. That commission brought together the Pee Dee, the Catawba, the Santee, the Four Holes Indian Association, the Chicora-Waccamaw, and the Piedmont Indian Association. Governor Beasley later rescinded that agreement, deciding on the recommendation of legal counsel to reaffirm the old Palmetto Indian Affairs Commission instead.

In 2001, the Pee Dee of Dillon County incorporated as a non-profit corporation under the guidance of Chief Carolyn Chavis-Bolton as the Pee Dee Indian Nation of Upper South Carolina. This marked a return to the Pee Dee tradition of women as chiefs and war captains seen in Colonial times.

Due to European prejudices against dealing with women in the 18th and 19th centuries, leadership of the Pee Dee had been taken by a succession of male tribal elders within each of the disparate communities. This gender bias has become commonplace among Indian tribes.

1MISSIONERS OF THE SC INDIAN AFFAIRS COMMISSION ©GENE CRE
THE STATE HOUSE, 2007

The Pee Dee Indian Nation of Upper South Carolina led by Chief Carolyn Chavis-Bolton, along with the Waccamaw became the first Indian tribes officially recognized by the State of South Carolina. No branch of the Pee Dee tribe is recognized by the United States Federal government. However, many bands of the original tribe are now listed as state recognized tribes or groups by the state of South Carolina..

The only tribe in South Carolina that has regained United States federal recognition is the closely-related Catawba tribe. The Pee Dee Indian Nation of Upper South Carolina filed a Notice of Intent with the Bureau of Indian Affairs in 2008 and is seeking Federal recognition.

Epilogue

The descendants of the historic tribe are currently split into several different tribes with members living mostly in South Carolina, North Carolina, and Georgia. These tribes are the Pee Dee Nation of Upper South Carolina (recognized in 2005)), the Beaver Creek Indians (http://www.beavercreekindians.org/), the Pee Dee Indian Tribe of South Carolina (http://www.peedeeindiantribeofsc.com/), and the Pee Dee Indian Nation of Beaver Creek (http://www.peedeeindiannation.com/). There are presently a number of political tensions between the groups which hinders the reconciliation and reunion of the bands

This book was written to document the struggles of the Pee Dee Indians of the Southeast. They have endured for centuries under an apartheid system almost as cruel as that of South Africa. Despite this they have continued to struggle to maintain their unique heritage and traditions in an often hostile world.

From adopting the Mississippian culture to adopting the European culture, from fighting with their nearest neighbors in every war to working alongside those neighbors in times of peace, the Pee Dee have always shown the ability to adapt and survive when many Indian people did not. Today, the Pee Dee still farm their lands, work side by side with non-Indians and serve in the country's defense in any conflict while continuing to govern and care for themselves to the best of their abilities. They have stopped hiding in plain sight and are now fighting for their rights and trying to preserve their environment and lands.[115]

Appendix A: The Town Creek Ceremonial Center

High on a bluff overlooking the juncture of Town Creek and Little River the Indians of the Pee Dee established a ceremonial center. Here people from every village converged for political, religious, and social activities. The Town Creek ceremonial center served as a place for discussion of matters of importance to the collective clans of the tribe, as well as the setting for important religious ceremonies and feasts often lasting several days. Here, too, the socially important dead were buried, enemies were ceremoniously put to death during celebrations of victory after battle, and exciting ball games between warriors of competing towns were played. There were no occupants living within the walls of the stockade compound, except for the priests in charge.

The palisade surrounding the Town Creek center was constructed of upright logs interwoven with cane and small poles, plastered with a mixture of clay and straw. Entrance to the enclosure was gained through two protective towers, one on the north and one on the south, as well as via an underground passage from the river. The palisade served as a fortified refuge from the Siouan tribes in the area who sought to reconquer the lands of their ancestors. Within these protective walls, on a slight rise on the western side, stood the principal structure--an earthen mound constructed of dirt carried there in baskets on the backs of people from surrounding towns. The mound was built in stages. At first, there was a ceremonial earth lodge, which in time collapsed. More earth was placed on the mound, and upon this foundation a new rectangular structure was erected. When this building burned, a final mantle of earth was placed over it. Upon this last addition to the mound were found the archaeological remains of the third and last structure to be built--the major temple.

The temple, which was the most important building within the enclosure, was thatched with bundles of grass. Inside, the mud-plastered walls were decorated with paintings. Seats were arranged around the inside wall; village chiefs and the bravest of the warriors sat here. The Indians were sun worshippers who correlated the sun with fire; a fire laid in a pit at the center of the temple always was kept burning.

Symbolically, each of the four logs on the fire faced one of the cardinal points of the compass. The temple contained an altar which held sacred objects used by the priests. A reconstruction of the major temple is located on the summit of the mound.

In front of the ramp leading to the top of the mound were four sheds facing each other and forming a square plot of ground between them. Known as the "square ground" this area was considered sacred, for on it dwelt the Talwa, or symbolic soul of the tribe. Each shed was decorated with symbols of the clans which occupied them, including carvings, paintings, scalps, and war clubs. Members of the clans were assigned places in the sheds, and seating was according to tribal rank or station. The men of the tribe met in this place to discuss and settle matters concerning politics and religion.

A large ball post used as a goal in a variety of games stood beside the square ground, the skull of a bear hanging from its top. Warriors from the villages formed competing teams and often would play strenuous ball games around the post in a demonstration of their strength and courage. The game contained elements of today's games of lacrosse, football, and soccer. Ball games were second only to warfare as a way in which a warrior could distinguish himself and gain honors.

Outside the ball grounds were round thatch-roofed huts where the dead were buried; other mortuaries were located near the square ground. Across the plaza, within a square compound next to the river, stood a minor temple, its basic form similar to that of the major temple. All ceremonial structures were rectangular, fashioned with walls of wattle and daub and roofs of thatch. Enclosed by a palisade of small logs, it served as a dwelling for the priests in charge of ceremonies. The minor temple, too, has been rebuilt where the original was located.

Ceremonies in the temple consisted of pipe smoking, feasting, drinking, singing, and entertainment, frequently lasting all night. Women were seldom allowed to take part in ceremonies in either the square ground or the temple; at times groups of them provided entertainment in the form of dancing. Prior to meetings in the temple, a sacred brew, known as the "Black drink" was taken by the participants as a stimulant to the mind and body.

The Poskito, or renewal ceremony, was the most important of several ceremonies to be held in the square ground during the year. Known by the White man as the ceremony of the "busk," deriving from the Indian word meaning "a fast," it also was referred to as the "green corn ceremony," as corn played an important part in the ritual performed. The eight day celebration was held after the gathering of the first new corn crop, to mark the beginning the new year.

To prepare for the busk, Indians of the villages cleaned and swept their houses, sprinkling them with clean sand. They discarded old clothing, pottery, and implements, replacing those things with newly fashioned ones. The ceremonial center, too, was cleaned, and the temple and grounds repaired. All fires were extinguished. All debts and grievances were settled; all unpunished crimes except murder were forgiven. All was made ready to begin the new year with the eating of the new corn. During the first four days of the busk, people from the surrounding villages gathered at the Town Creek ceremonial center to take part in rituals of purification. These included ceremonial bathing, fasting, scratching the body with a gar fish tooth or sharp stone to expel evil spirits, and taking cathartic medicines. The most famous of these medicines, the Black drink, was made from the leaves of the yaupon shrub. After the leaves were parched in pots and then steeped in boiling water, the resultant Black liquid was served to participants in whom it induced violent vomiting, thus cleansing the individual of inner evil.

The second part of the busk was a period of feasting and celebration. It began with a ceremonial rekindling of the sacred fire; Indians returning to their villages at the close of the busk carried embers from the new fire with which to relight the hearths in their homes. It was because of this sharing of the new fire by all the tribal members that the Indians of the Pee Dee culture referred to themselves as "people of one fire". After the lighting of the fire, which signified the start of a new year, four ears of the new corn were offered to the spirits; eating of the new corn, which had been forbidden during the first part of the busk, was now allowed. At this time, the young men of the tribe who had reached and proven their manhood during the preceding year were given warrior names; they then were privileged to participate in all adult activities of the tribe, including making homes of their own.[116]

Appendix B: South Carolina Slave Code

An Act for the better Ordering and Governing [of] Negroes and other Slaves in this Province

Whereas in his majesty's plantations in America, slavery has been introduced and allowed; and the people commonly called negroes, Indians, mulattoe and Mestizos have [been] deemed absolute slaves, and the subjects of property in the hands of particular persons the extent of whose power over slaves ought to be settled and limited by positive laws so that the slaves may be kept in due subjection and obedience, and the owners and other persons having the care and government of slaves, may be restrained from exercising too great rigor and cruelty over them; and that the public peace and order of this Province may be preserved:

Be it enacted, that all negroes, Indians (free Indians in amity with this government, and negroes, mulattoe and Mestizos who are now free excepted) mulattoe or Mestizos who now are or shall hereafter be in this Province, and all their issue and offspring born or to be born, shall be and they are hereby declared to be and remain forever hereafter absolute slaves, and shall follow the condition of the mother; and shall be deemed, … taken, reputed and adjudged in law to be chattels personal in the hands of their owners and possessors and their executors, administrators and assigns to all intents, constructions and purposes whatsoever, Provided that if any negro Indian mulattoe, or Mestizos shall claim his or her freedom, it shall and may be lawful for such negro, Indian, mulattoe, or Mestizos, or any person or persons whatsoever, on his or her behalf to apply to the justices of his Majesty's court of common pleas by petition or motion, either during the sitting of the said court, or before any of the justices of the same court at any time in the vacation. And the said court or any of the justices thereof, shall and they are hereby fully empowered to admit any person so applying, to be guardian for any negro, Indian, mulattoe or Mestizos, claiming his, her or their freedom, and such guardians shall be enabled, entitled and capable in law to bring an action of trespass, in the nature of ravishment of ward against any person who shall claim property in, or who shall be in possession of any such negro, Indian, mulattoe or Mestizos.

Provided that in any action or suit to be brought in pursuance of the direction of this act the burthen of the proof shall lay upon the plaintiff, and it shall be always presumed, that every negro, Indian, mulattoe, and Mestizos, is a slave unless the contrary can be made appear (the Indians in amity with this government excepted) in which case the burden of the proof shall lie on the defendant.

III. And for the better keeping slaves in due order and subjection: be it further enacted that no person whatsoever, shall permit or suffer any slave under his or their care or management, and who lives, or is employed in Charlestown, or any other town in this Province to go out of the limits of the said town, or any such slave, who lives in the country to go out of the plantation to which such slave belongs, or in which plantation such slave is usually employed, without a letter subscribed and directed, or a ticket in the words following... .

V. If any slave who shall be out of the house or plantation where such slave shall live or shall be usually employed, or without some White person in company with such slave, shall refuse to submit or to undergo the examination of any White person, it shall be lawful for any such White Person to pursue, apprehend and moderately correct such slave; and if such slave shall assault and strike such White person, such slave may be lawfully killed.

IX. And whereas natural justice forbids, that any person of what condition soever should be condemned unheard, and the order of civil government requires that for the due and equal administration of justice, some convenient method and form of trial should be established, Be it therefore enacted, that all crimes and offences which shall be committed by slaves in this Province and for which capital punishment shall or lawfully may be inflicted, shall be heard, examined, tried, adjudged, and finally determined by any 2 justices assigned to keep the peace, and any number of freeholders not less than 3 or more than 5 in the county where the offence shall be committed and can be most conveniently assembled; either of which justices, on complaint made or information received of any such offence committed by a slave, shall commit the offender to the safe custody of the constable of the parish where such offence shall be committed, and shall without delay by warrant under his hand and seal, call to his assistance, and request any one of the nearest justices of the peace to associate with him; and shall by the same warrant summon such a number of the neighboring freeholders as aforesaid, to assemble and meet together with the said justices, at a certain day and place not exceeding 3 days after the apprehending of such slave or slaves: and the justices and freeholders being so assembled, shall cause the slave accused or charged, to be brought before them, and shall hear the accusations which shall be brought against such slave, and his or her defence, and shall proceed to the examination of witnesses, and other evidence, and finally hear and determine the matter brought before them, in the most summary and expeditious manner; and in case the offender shall be convicted of any crime for which by law the offender ought to suffer death, the said justices shall give judgment, and award and cause execution of their sentence to be done, by inflicting such manner of death, and at such time as the said justices, by and with the consent of the freeholders shall direct, and which they shall judge will be most effectual to deter others from offending in the like manner.

[XVI.] Be it therefore enacted, that the several crimes and offences hereinafter particularly enumerated, are hereby declared to be felony without the benefit of the clergy, That is to say, If any slave, free negro, mulatto, Indian, or Mestizos, shall willfully and maliciously burn or destroy any stack of rice, corn or other grain, of the product, growth or manufacture of this Province; or shall willfully and maliciously set fire to, burn or destroy any tar kiln, barrels of pitch, tar, turpentine or rosin, or any other of the goods or commodities of the growth, produce or manufacture of this Province; or shall feloniously steal, take or carry away any slave, being the property of another, with intent to carry such slave out of this Province; or shall willfully and maliciously poison, or administer any poison to any person, free man, woman, servant or slave; every such slave, free negro, mulatto, Indian (except as before excepted) and Mestizos, shall suffer death as a felon.

XVII. Any slave who shall be guilty of homicide of any sort, upon any White person, except by misadventure or in defence of his master or other person under whose care and government such slave shall be, shall upon conviction thereof as aforesaid, suffer death. And every slave who shall raise or attempt to raise an insurrection in this Province, or shall endeavor to delude or entice any slave to run away and leave this Province; every such slave and slaves, and his and their accomplices, aiders and abettors, shall upon conviction as aforesaid suffer death. Provided always, That it shall and may be lawful to and for the justices who shall pronounce sentence against such slaves, and by and with the advice and consent of the freeholders as aforesaid, if several slaves shall receive sentence at one time, to mitigate and alter the sentence of any slave other than such as shall be convicted of the homicide of a White person, who they shall think may deserve mercy, and may inflict such corporal punishment (other than death) on any such slave, as they in their discretion shall think fit, any thing herein contained to the contrary thereof in any wise notwithstanding. Provided, That one or more of the said slaves who shall be convicted of the crimes or offences aforesaid, where several are concerned, shall be executed for example, to deter others from offending in the like kind.

XXXIII. And whereas several owners of slaves do suffer their slaves to go and work where they please, upon condition of paying to their owners certain sums of money agreed upon between the owner and slave; which practice occasioned such slaves to pilfer and steal to raise money for their owners, as well as to maintain themselves in drunkenness and evil courses; for prevention of which practices for the future, Be it enacted, that no owner, master or mistress of any slave, after the passing of this act, shall permit or suffer any of his, her or their slaves to go and work out of their respective houses or families, without a ticket in writing under pain of forfeiting the sum of current money, for every such offence.

XXXVI. And for that as it is absolutely necessary to the safety of this Province, that all due care be taken to restrain the wanderings and meetings of negroes and other slaves, at all times, and more especially on Saturday nights, Sundays and other holidays, and the using and carrying wooden swords, and other mischievous and dangerous weapons, or using and keeping of drums, horns, or other loud instruments, which may call together or give sign or notice to one another of their wicked designs and purposes; and that all masters, overseers and others may be enjoined diligently and carefully to prevent the same, Be it enacted, that it shall be lawfull for all masters, overseers and other persons whomsoever, to apprehend and take up any negro or other slave that shall be found out of the plantation of his or their master or owner, at any time, especially on Saturday nights, Sundays or other holidays, not being on lawful business, and with a letter from their master or a ticket, or not having a White person with them, and the said negro or other slave or slaves correct by a moderate whipping.

XXXVII. And whereas cruelty is not only highly unbecoming those who profess themselves Christians, but is odious in the eyes of all men who have any sense of virtue or humanity; therefore to restrain and prevent barbarity being exercised toward slaves, Be it enacted, That if any person or persons whosoever, shall willfully murder his own slave, or the slave of another person, every such person shall upon conviction thereof, forfeit and pay the sum of £700 current money, and shall be rendered, and is hereby declared altogether and forever incapable of holding, exercising, enjoying or receiving the profits of any office, place or employment civil or military within this Province: … And if any person shall on a sudden heat of passion, or by undue correction, kill his own slave or the slave of any person, he shall forfeit the sum of £350 current money, And in case any person or persons shall wilfully cut out the tongue, put out the eye, castrate or cruelly scald, burn, or deprive any slave of any limb or member, or shall inflict any other cruel punishment, other than by whipping or beating with a horsewhip, cow-skin, switch or small stick, or by putting irons on, or confining or imprisoning such slave; every such person shall for every such offence, forfeit the sum of £100 current money.

XXXVIII. That in case any person in this Province, who shall be owner, or who shall have the care government or charge of any slave, or slaves, shall deny, neglect or refuse to allow such slave or slaves under his or her charge, sufficient cloathing, covering or food, it shall and may be lawfull for any person or persons, on behalf of such slave or slaves, to make complaint to the next neighboring justice in the parish where such slave or slaves live, or are usually employed; and if there shall be no justice in the parish, then to the next justice in nearest parish: and the said justice shall summon the party against whom such complaint shall be made, and shall enquire of, hear and determine the same: and if the said justice shall find the said complaint to be true, or that such person will not exculpate or clear himself from the charge, by his or her own oath, which such person shall be at liberty to do in all cases where positive proof is not given of the offence, such justice shall and may make such orders upon the same for the relief of such slave or slaves, as he in his discretion shall think fit, and shall and may let and impose a fine or penalty on any person who shall offend in the premises, in any sum not exceeding £20 current money, for each offence.

XLIV. And whereas many owners of slaves, and others who have the care, management and overseeing of slaves, do confine them so closely to hard labour; that they have not sufficient time for natural rest—Be it therefore enacted, That if any owner of slaves, or other person who shall have the care, management, or overseeing of any slaves, shall work or put any such slave or slaves to labour, more than 15 hours in 24 hours, from the 25th day of March to the 25th day of September, or more than 14 hours in 24 hours, from the 25th day of September to the 25th day of March; every such person shall forfeit any sum not exceeding or under £20, nor under £5 current money, for every time he, she or they shall offend herein, at the discretion of the justice before whom the complaint shall be made.

XLV. And whereas the having of slaves taught to write, or suffering them to be employed in writing, may be attended with great inconveniences; Be it enacted, that all and every person and persons whatsoever, who shall hereafter teach, or cause any slave or slaves to be taught to write, or shall use or employ any slave as a scribe in any manner of writing whatsoever, hereafter taught to write; every such person and persons shall, for every such offence, forfeit the sum of £100 current money.[117]

Appendix C: Burnt Swamp Baptist Association

Many members of the tribe began assimilation into White society, helping to avoid removal to present-day Oklahoma in the early 19th Century. The legacy of this assimilation led to a number of issues in the 20th Century. During segregation, it was seen as advantageous to identify as "White." Since many Pee Dee were already of mixed ancestry, people began to pass in order to make their day to day lives easier. Currently, a combination of Methodist and Native American Church religions is observed there. Many Pee Dee people are buried in their historic cemeteries.

Burnt Swamp Association began in 1877 with four original member churches and today consists of 64 churches and 4 missions. The association bears uniqueness in that churches are comprised largely of Native American members. Several tribal groups affiliate with the association: Haliwa-Saponi in Warren and Halifax counties; Lumbee in Robeson and surrounding counties and Baltimore, MD; Pee Dee in South Carolina; Coharie in Sampson County; Waccamaw-Siouan in Bladen and Columbus counties; and some Tuscarora in the Robeson county area.

 Bi-vocational pastors lead 80% of the churches. All but two of the 69 churches are led by Native American pastors from tribes of this region. Indigenous lay and clergy leaders serve not only the churches but also are vital to general community political and social life.

Early settlers brought their faith with them; they found a receptive audience in Indian communities. Presbyterians and Methodists, and then Baptists, brought the gospel message to Indian people in Carolina. By the start of the nineteenth century, the witness of White Baptists spread in the region and their numbers increased.

Endnotes

---

[1] U.S. Census Bureau, "Profile and General Demographic Characteristics, Table DP – 1, 2000.

[2] Theda Perdue, American Indian Survival, The South Carolina Historical Magazine, Volume 108, Number 3, July 2007.

[3] Frank G. Speck, "Siouan Tribes of the Carolinas as Known from Catawba, Tutelo and Documentary Sources", American Anthropologist, Volume 37 published in 1935, pages 202, 221.

[4] Hudson, The .Juan Pardo Expeditions. p. 76.

[5] Instead of encompassing a duality of sacred and profane, Native American religious traditions conceive only of sacred and more sacred. Spirit or power moves in all things, though not equally. For native communities religion is understood as the relationship between living humans and other persons or things, however they are conceived. These may include departed as well as yet-to-be-born human beings, beings in the so-called "natural world" of flora and fauna, and visible entities that are not animate by Western standards, such as mountains, springs, lakes, and clouds. This group of entities also includes what scholars of religion might denote as "mythic beings," beings that are not normally visible but are understood to inhabit and affect either this world or some other contiguous to it.

[6] Joseph Epes Brown, "The Spiritual Legacy of the American Indian", Crossroad, New York, 1982, pages. 1 - 4.

[7] Keith H. Basso, "Wisdom Sits in Places", University of New Mexico Press, Albuquerque, 1996.

[8] Joseph Epes Brown, "The Spiritual Legacy of the American Indian", Crossroad, New York, 1982, pages 63-64.

[9] http://www.firstpeople.us/FP-Html-Legends/Legends-PS.html.

[10] *Did First Americans Arrive By Land and Sea?* Hillary Mayell for National Geographic News. November 6, 2003.

[11] The State Newspaper.

[12] V. Havard. Food Plants of the North American Indians. *Bulletin of the Torrey Botanical Club*, Vol. 22, No. 3 (Mar. 27, 1895), pp. 98-123. Published by: Torrey Botanical Society. http://www.jstor.org/stable/2477757 .

[13] Photograph by author. Town Creek Mound. 2009.

[14] Dragonwagon, Crescent (2007). *The Cornbread Gospels*. Workman Publishing. ISBN 0-7611-1916-7.

[15] Hudson, Charles. "A Conquered People". *The Southeastern Indians*. The University of Tennessee Press. p. 498-499.

[16] Charles Hudson, *The Juan Pardo Expeditions: Exploration of the Carolinas and Tennessee, 1566-1568* (Tuscaloosa, 1990, reprint 2005).

[17] Charles Hudson, *The Juan Pardo Expeditions: Exploration of the Carolinas and Tennessee, 1566-1568* (Tuscaloosa, 1990, reprint 2005).

[18] David G. Moore, "Pardo Expeditions" in William S. Powell, ed., *Encyclopedia of North Carolina* (Chapel Hill, 2006).

[19] Hudson, The .Juan Pardo Expeditions. p. 76.

[20] Hudson, The Juan Pardo Expeditions, p. 78

[21] (Coe, p. 308-309).

[22] Hudson, The Juan Pardo Expeditions, p. 53.

[23] Hudson, The Catawba Nation, p. 26.

[24] Hudson, The Juan Pardo Expeditions, p. 58.

[25] Hudson, The Juan Pardo Expeditions, p. 55.

[26] *Cherokee Women: Gender and Culture Change, 1700-1835*. Lincoln: University of Nebraska Press, 1998.

[27] Hudson, The Juan Pardo Expeditions, p. 59.

[28] Hudson, The .Juan Pardo Expeditions, p. 59.

[29]. Hudson, The Juan Pardo Expeditions, p. 55.

[30] Hudson, The Juan Pardo Expeditions, p. 55.

[31] Hudson, <u>The .Juan Pardo Expeditions. p</u>. 58.

[32] Hudson, <u>The Juan Pardo Expeditions, p</u>. 72.

[33]DePratter, Chester B. Santa Elena Project, The South Carolina Institute of Archaeology and Anthropology. 19 April 2009 www.cas.sc.edu/sciaa/staff/depratterc/newweb.htm

[34] The eight "Lords Proprietors" were:

- Lord Chancellor EDWARD HYDE CLARENDON, (1st Earl of Clarendon & Prime Minister),
- Sir GEORGE MONCK, (1st Duke of Albemarle, General Monck),
- Lord CRAVEN,
- Lord JOHN BERKELEY, of New Jersey,
- Lord ANTHONY ASHLEY COOPER, (1st Earl of Shaftesbury),
- Sir GEORGE CARTERET, of New Jersey,
- Sir WILLIAM BERKELEY, (Governor of Virginia), and
- Sir JOHN COLLETON.

[35] Iner, Charles. History of South Carolina Land Surveying.

[36] Milling, p. 220.

[37] Mooney, James. The Siouan Tribes of the East. Washington, D.C.: U.S. Government Printing Office, 1894.

[38] Swanton, <u>Indians...,</u> p. 203.

[39] Galloway, Patricia Kay.. : Practicing ethnohistory: mining archives, hearing testimony, constructing narrative / Patricia Galloway. Lincoln: University of Nebraska Press, 2006.

[40] Gallay, Alan. "Forgotten Story of Indian Slavery" (2003).

[41] Gallay, Alan. *The Indian Slave Trade: The Rise of the English Empire in the American South, 1670-1717*. New Haven, Yale University Press, 2002.

[42] Gallay, Alan. *The Indian Slave Trade: The Rise of the English Empire in the American South, 1670-1717*. New Haven, Yale University Press, 2002.

[43] From the indexed, 1967, UNC Press edition, called <u>A New Voyage to Carolina</u>, of a book published by John Lawson in London in 1709.

[44] Barnwell, p. 393-396, Milling, p. 118.

[45] Virginia Magazine, p. 392-394.

[46] <u>Journals of the Commissioners of the Indian Trade</u>, September 20, 1710 – August 29, 1718, Columbia, South Carolina Archives Department, 1955, page 96, from a set of instructions, dated July 3lst, 1716, from the Commissioners to a trader they had just licensed. / British Public Records Office, Records Relating to South Carolina, Volume 6, pages 235-242, transcript in the S.C. Archives: a letter from Benjamin Godin, Ralph Izard and Edward Hyrne, to someone in England, dated August 6th, 1716.

[47] S.C. Public Records, VII, p. 236-238.

[48] Swanton, <u>History Quarterly,</u> p. 101-102.

[49] Phillips, Paul and J.W. Smurr. *The Fur Trade.* 2 vols. Norman, Oklahoma: University of Oklahoma Press, 1961.

[50] Council Journal Green Copy August 25, 1671-July 11, 1721, page 122, S.C. Archives.

[51] Council Journal Green Copy August 25, 1671-July 11. 1721, page 122, S.C. Archives.

[52] See page 46 History of the Kusso

[53] Petitions for Land from SC Council Journals Vol. I, 1734/5 - 1748, page 95.

[54] Ozato, date of June 6th, 1759, apparently the first Catawba King whose name we know since Wikmanata^si in 1719 (on page 29).

[55] Ozato, date of June 6th, 1759, apparently the first Catawba King whose name we know since Wikmanata^si in 1719 (on page 29).

[56] A list (numbered up to page 55 but including a dozen blank pages) made by John Hammerton, Secretary of the Province, of public documents issued by him during the first one-third of his thirty years in office (1752 to 1762). Inexplicably bound into the front of: Inventories, Book LL (1744-1746), S.C. Archives.

---

[57] Commons House Journal f5, page 74, S.C. Archives: In Charleston on April 20th, 1716, "Having examined the" old "Waccamaw Indian" man "by Mr. Waties' interpretation, we find that" the Englishman, "Mr. Waties, does not understand the same, nor can speak the" Waccamaw "language, but only the Pedee" tongue. "So we are as much in the dark as ever." - Thus the Peedee Indians did not speak the Woccon language of which we have a 150-word vocabulary.

[58] On May 5rd, 1755, the King of the Catawba Nation (King Hagler) told the Council in Charleston "that in carrying the Commission he had received from his Excellency, in the rain, it had received so much damage that it could not new be read."

[59] Council Journal, British Public Records Office Photostats #2, June 8th, 15th, S.C. Archives. Colonial Plate, Volume 2, page 430, and Volume 4, page 229; S.C. Archives.

[60] Council Journal #7, pages 116-117 (March 25th, 1758), S.C. Archives. Charleston Deeds. S, pages 190-192 (March 27th & 28th, 1758. with a plat), S.C. Archives. J.H. Easterby, editor. The Journal of the Commons House of Assembly November 10th, 1756-June 7th, 1759 (Columbia, S.C.. 1951), pages 565-566 (March 25th, 1758).

[61] J.H. Easterby, editor. Journal of the Commons House of Assembly September 12th. 1759-March 26th, 1741 (Columbia, S.C., 1952), page 185, account #6 (February 6th, 1740 New Style).

[62] Secretary Hammerton says that he spent £3 on March 6th, 1742 to have made "A Special Commission for Billy Waites to be King of the Peedees over Santee river, in room of King Harry or Pinch." And a pound and 10 shillings on one for or "To Captain Billy, Chief Captain under King Billy."

[63] "King Will" and his "Chief Captain," Johnny, "of the Peedees over the four Hole Swamp", together with King Billy Waites and his "Chief Captain," repetitiously called Captain Billy, "of the Peedees over Santee river," all four Conmissions date of March 6th, 1742.

[64] Council Journal #21, Part Two, page 404 (April 21st, 1755), S.C. Archives.

[65] The original SOOkiree Town in the Catawba Nation on Sugar creek (the name means "House Strong" in Catawba) is represented in Hammerton's tally by: "Captain Harris of Sugar Town" (Oct. 23rd, 1759, page 29); "Captain Jeamy Harris of Old Sugar Town" (April 29th, 1741); "Suger Jemmy" or Pick Ahassokehee (September 4th, 1749'). and "Captain Harris" or "Captain Jemmy" (December 23rd. 1749, more or less when he died). – The other Catawba Town with about the same name existed not in the Catawba Nation from 1712 to 1756 but instead as a geographical sister town to the Waxhaw nation, at Landsford Shoals on Catawba river (1715 map, 1756 map)

and next to St. Augustine, Florida (1719). Returned to the Catawba Nation, this small branch hamlet shows up there under "Captain Peter of Sutrea Town" on October 23rd, 1759, and under "Captain Jack of Soutry Town" from 1741 to 1744, when he got killed. SOOkiree = "fort strong" SOOtiree = "downstream, south" (Dr, Siehert – sukiri', sutiri)

[66] Council Journal #ll, pages 425-428 (July 25th, 1744, including the letter of the 23rd), S.C. Archives.

[67] Council Journal #ll, pages 425-428 (July 25th, 1744, including the letter of the 23rd), S.C. Archives.

[68] Council Journal #ll, pages 425-428 (July 25th, 1744, including the letter of the 23rd), S.C. Archives.

[69] Council Journal #ll, pages 425-428 (July 25th, 1744, including the letter of the 23rd), S.C. Archives.

[70] S.C. Public Records, p. 414.

[71] Gregg, p. 13.

[72] Rights, D. *"The American Indian In North Carolina."* Durham, NC: Duke University Publications. 1947.

[73] Gallay, Alan (2002). The Indian Slave Trade: The Rise of the English Empire in the American South 1670-1717. Yale University Press. ISBN 0-300-10193-7

[74] Milton Ready, *The Tar Heel State: A History of North Carolina* (Columbia, 2005).

[75] Colonial Records, V. I, p. 85; Brown, p. 172.

[76] Colonial Records, V. I, p. 166.

[77] Colonial Records, Vol. I, p. 362.

[78] Brown, p. 224.

[79] Gregg, p. 16.

[80] Commons House Journals, Sainsbury Copy, pages 1,018-1,019, S.C. Archives. Alexander Gregg could not include this reference in his book, <u>History of the Old Cheraws</u>, in 1867, because the only surviving copy was in England.

[81] Swanton, <u>Indians...,</u> p. 203.

[82] Brown, p. 23, Milling, p. 229.

[83] Colonial Records, V. II, p. 85.

[84] Colonial Records, V. II, 85-87.

[85] A Journal of the Proceedings of John Evans to the Catawbaw Nation begun Oct. 14th, 1755 by Order of his Excellency.

[86] BPRD, Vols. 21, pages 399 - 406, South Carolina Archives. Page 401 - 402.

[87] . "Robin, Chief Warrior of the Peedees near Four Holes", March 19th, 1745 (on Hammerton's page 55).

[88] William L. McDowell, Jr., editor. Colonial Records of South Carolina: DOCUMENTS RELATING TO INDIAN AFFAIRS May 21st, 1750-August 7th, 1754 (Columbia, S.C., 1958), page 576.

[89] Council Journal #ll, pages 425-428 (July 25th, 1744, including the letter of the 23rd), S.C. Archives.

[90] Records relating to South Carolina in the British Public Records Office, Volume 21, pages 599-406 (a letter to England from Governor Glen in Charleston, S.C., September 22nd, 1744), particularly page 401; S.C. Archives.

[91] See R. M. Brown, *The South Carolina Regulators* (1963).

[92] Calloway, Colin G. *The American Revolution in Indian Country: Crisis and Diversity in Native American Communities.* (Melbourne, Australia: Cambridge University Press, 1995.)

[93] *Rangers In Colonial And Revolutionary America.* US Army Center For Military History.

[94] Brown, p. 262.

[95] Audited Accounts, No.91.

[96] Brown, p.262.

[97] Audited Accounts, No.91.

[98] Milling, p. 230.

[99] See *Chavis Family Book* for genealogical information.

[100] Edgar, Walter B. *South Carolina: A History*. Columbia, SC: University of South Carolina Press, 1998.

[101] Hauptman, Laurence M. *Between Two Fires: American Indians in the Civil War.* New York. The Free Press (Simon and Schuster), 1995.

[102] Three indentured servants—John Punch, James Gregory, and Victor —ran away and were recaptured. James Gregory and Victor, both white, were given "thirty stripes" and an additional four years of servitude, whereas John Punch, a Negro, was sentenced to serve the remainder of his life. Helen Tunnicliff Catterall, ed., *Judicial Cases Concerning American Slavery and the Negro,* 5 vols. (1926; reprint, New York: Octagon Books, 1968; KF4545.S5 C3 1968), 1:77.

[103] *Celia, a Slave* is a narrative account of such a criminal trial, where a slave woman was tried for the murder of her owner, found guilty, and sentenced to be hanged. Robert Newsom, age sixty, had purchased Celia, age fourteen, to be his live-in mistress. Five years later, she asked him to discontinue sexual relations with her until after the birth of their second child. He refused and she killed him by beating him with a piece of wood and burned his body in her fireplace. She could not testify on her own behalf because that would have meant permitting a black person to bring evidence against a white person. Melton A. McLaurin, *Celia, a Slave* (Athens: University of Georgia Press, 1991; KF223.C43 M34 1991)

[104] Catterall, Helen Tunnicliff. *Judicial Cases concerning American Slavery and the Negro.* 5 vols. Reprint, New York: Octagon Books, 1968 (KF4545.S5 C3 1968).

[105] Sider, Gerald. Living Indian Histories: The Lumbee and Tuscarora People in North Carolina.

[106] Mee, Arthur; Hammerton, J. A.; Innes, Arthur D., "Harmsworth history of the world, Volume 4", 1907, Carmelite House, London

[107] http://www.digitalhistory.uh.edu/database/article_display.cfm?HHID=130

[108] History of Dillon County, p. 267.

[109] The Dillon, S.C. Herald, February 24, 2005, "Recognition at Last"..

[110] The Dillon, S.C. Herald, February 24, 2005, "Recognition at Last"..

[111] Charleston, S.C. News & Courier, June 3, 1968, "Dillon Indian School Is Joining the Jet Age."

[112] From interviews with residents of Little Rock, S.C. conducted by author.

[113] The buildings still stand and are occupied although in very poor condition.

[114] Theda Perdue, *American Indian Survival in South Carolina.* The South Carolina historical magazine, volume 108, number 3, July 2007.

[115] Photograph by Chief Carolyn Chavis-Bolton

[116] Extracted from *Time before History: The Archaeology of North Carolina*, by H. Trawick Ward and R. P. Stephen Davis Jr., University of North Carolina Press, 1999.

[117] Mee, Arthur; Hammerton, J. A.; Innes, Arthur D., "Harmsworth history of the world, Volume 4", 1907, Carmelite House, London; (at section: "Social Fabric of the Ancient World, IV": in article: William Romaine Paterson: "The effects of the slave system: man's inhumanity to man it's own retribution"); at page 2834; where the author cites this excerpt from the South Carolina Black Code after saying: "Christian slave states in the nineteenth century passed laws which are identical in spirit and almost in letter with the slave laws of Babylon. We saw that in Babylon death was the penalty for anyone who assisted a slave to escape. The Code declared that ' if a man has induced either a male or female slave from the house of a patrician or plebeian to leave the city, he shall be put to death.'"

Works Cited

1.   "First People - The Legends." First People - The Legends. N.p., 19 Apr 2009. Web. 19 Feb 2011. <http://www.firstpeople.us/>.

2.   Alexander, Gregg. History of the Old Cheraws. 1st. New York, NY: Richardson and Company, 1867. Print.

3.   Basso, Keith H.   "Wisdom Sits in Places."   Albuquerque: University of New Mexico Press, 1996. Print.

4.   Brown, Joseph Epes. "The Spiritual Legacy of the American Indian." New York: Crossroad, 1982. Print.

5.   Carroll, B.R. "Historical Collections of South Carolina." New York: Harper and Brothers. 1836. Print.

6.   Deloria, Jr., Vine. "God Is Red: A Native View of Religion." Golden, Colorado: Fulcrum Publishing. 2003. Print.

7.   DePratter, Chester B. Santa Elena Project, The South Carolina Institute of Archaeology and Anthropology. 19 April 2009 www.cas.sc.edu/sciaa/staff/depratterc/newweb.htm.

8.   Documents Relating to Indian Affairs. Colonial Records of South Carolina. Columbia: South Carolina Archives Department, 1958. Print.

9.   Dragonwagon, Crescent. "The Cornbread Gospels." New York. Workman Publishing Company. 2007. Print.

10.   Gallay, Alan. "Forgotten Story of Indian Slavery." 1st. New Haven: Yale University Press. 2003. Print.

11.   Gallay, Alan. The Indian Slave Trade: The Rise of the English Empire in the American South, 1670-1717. 1st. New Haven: Yale University Press. 2002. Print.

12.   Galloway, Patricia Kay. "Practicing Ethnohistory: Mining Archives, Hearing Testimony, Constructing Narrative." Lincoln: University of Nebraska Press. 2006. Print.

13.   Goodyear, A.C. Evidence of Pre-Clovis Sites in the Eastern United States" Paleoamerican Origins: Beyond Clovis. 1st. Austin: A&M University Press, 2005. Print.

14.   Gregg, Alexander. History of the old Cheraws, containing an account of the aborigines of the Pedee, the first white settlements, etc., extending from about A. D. 1730 to 1810, with notices of families and sketches of individuals; p. 15. New York, 1867. Print.

15.   Gross, David (ed.) We Won't Pay!: A Tax Resistance Reader ISBN 1434898253 pp. 77-79

16.   Hamilton, Jon Jay. Herman Husband: Penman of the Regulation. Graduate thesis. Wake Forest University, 1969.

17.   Havard, V. "Food Plants of the North American Indians." Bulletin of the Torrey Botanical Club. 22 (1895), pp. 98-123. Print.

18.   Hodge, Frederick Webb. "Handbook of the American Indians North of Mexico." New York: Pageant Books. 1959. Print.

19.   Hudson, Charles "The Juan Pardo Expeditions: Exploration of the Carolinas and Tennessee, 1566-1568". Washington, D.C.: Smithsonian Institution Press, 1990. Print.

20.   Hudson, Charles J. "The Catawba Nation." Athens, Georgia: University of Georgia Press. Print.

21.   Hudson, Charles. "A Conquered People". The Southeastern Indians. The University of Tennessee Press. p. 498-499. Print.

22.   Journals of the Commissioners of the Indian Trade. "Colonial Records of South Carolina." Columbia: South Carolina Archives Department, 1955. Print.

23.   Kars, Marjoleine. "Breaking Loose Together: The Regulator Rebellion in Pre-Revolutionary North Carolina." Chapel Hill: University of North Carolina Press, 2002. Print.

24.   Kay, Marvin L. M. "The North Carolina Regulation, 1766-1776: A Class Conflict." In The American Revolution: Explorations in the History of American Radicalism, edited by Alfred F. Young. DeKalb: Northern Illinois University Press, 1976. Print.

25.   Kay, Marvin L. M., and Lorin Lee Cary. "Class, Mobility, and Conflict in North Carolina on the Eve of the Revolution." In The Southern Experience in the American Revolution, edited by Jeffrey J. Crow and Larry E. Tise. Chapel Hill: University of North Carolina Press, 1978. Press.

26.   Lawson, John. A New Voyage to Carolina: containing the exact description and natural history of that country; together with the present state thereof; and a journal of a thousand miles, travel'd thro' several nations of Indians; giving a particular account of their customs, manners, etc. Chapel Hill: UNC Press. 1967. Print.

27.   Lawson, John. The history of Carolina, containing the exact description and natural history of that country, etc., p. 45. (Reprint from the London edition of 1714.) Raleigh, 1860. Print.

28.   Logan, J. "A History of the Upper Country of South Carolina - Vol. II." (Unpublished)

29.   Logan, J. "A History of the Upper Country of South Carolina: From the Earliest Periods to the Close of the War of Independence – Vol. I." Charleston, S.C.: S. G. Courtenay & Co. 1859. Print.

30.   Mayell, Hillary. Did First Americans Arrive By Land and Sea? National Geographic News. April 19, 2009. http://news.nationalgeographic.com/news/2003/11/1106_031106_firstamericans.html.

31.   McGee, W.J. "The Siouan Indians." 15th Annual Report, Bureau of America Ethnology. Washington, D.C.: U.S. Government Printing Office, 1897. Print.

32.   Mee, Arthur; Hammerton, J. A.; Innes, Arthur D., "Harmsworth history of the world, Volume 4." London: Carmelite House. 1907. Print.

33.   Mooney, James. "The Siouan Tribes of the East." Washington, D.C.: U.S. Government Printing Office. 1894. Print.

34.   Moore, David G. "Pardo Expeditions" Encyclopedia of North Carolina. Chapel Hill: University of North Carolna Press. 2006. Print.

35.   New York. Documents relative to the colonial history of the state of New York. Procured in Holland, England, and France, by John Romeyn Brodhead, etc. Edited by E. B. O'Callaghan, Glen (1751) and Albany Conference of 1751, vol. vi, p. 721. Albany, 1856-'77. 12 vols. Print.

36.   North Carolina. The Colonial Records of North Carolina, published under the supervision of the trustees of the public libraries, by order of the general assembly, Documents of 1715, vol. ii, pp. 251-2. Collected and edited by William L. Saunders, secretary of state. 10 vols. Raleigh, 1886-1890. Print.

37. O'Kelley, Patrick (2004). Nothing But Blood and Slaughter Military Operations and Order of Battle of the Revolutionary War in the Carolinas 1771-1779.

38. Parks, Douglas R.; & Rankin, Robert L. The Siouan languages. Handbook of North American Indians: Plains. 13. Washington, D.C.: Smithsonian Institution. Print.

39. Paul, Barbara Morningstar. "Native American Tribes and Groups in South Carolina." South Carolina Commission for Minority Affairs. South Carolina Commission for Minority Affairs. 19 Apr 2009. www.state.sc.us./cma/pdfs/maps_w_tribes.pdf.

40. Perdue, Theda. Cherokee Women: Gender and Culture Change, 1700-1835. Lincoln: University of Nebraska Press. 1998. Print.

41. Perdue, Theda. "American Indian Survival." The South Carolina Historical Magazine 108 (2007): pp. 1-10. Print.

42. Powell, William S., James K. Huhta, and Thomas J. Farnham (eds). The Regulators in North Carolina: A Documentary History. Raleigh: State Dept. of Archives and History, 1971. Print.

43. Rights, D. "The American Indian in North Carolina." Durham, NC: Duke University Publications. 1947. Print.

44. Sider, Gerald. "Living Indian Histories: The Lumbee and Tuscarora People in North Carolina." London, Chapel Hill: University of North Carolina Press. 2003. Print.

45. South Carolina Rivers Map - South Carolina Lake Map. Geology.com. 19 April 2009 geology.com/state-map/south-carolina.shtml.

46. Speck, Frank G. "Siouan Tribes of the Carolinas as Known from Catawba, Tutelo and Documentary Sources." American Anthropologist. 37 (1935): pp. 202-221. Print.

47. Stokes, Durwood T. "The History of Dillon County." Columbia, South Carolina: University of South Carolina Press. 1978. Print.

48. Taylor, Tom; Hunter, Eloise. "How the Indians Hunted and Fished." Wildlife in North Carolina. Raleigh, North Carolina State Museum of Natural Sciences. February, 1981. Print.

49. U.S. Census Bureau, "Profile and General Demographic Characteristics, Table DP – 1, 2000. 19 April 2009. http://www.bedfordoh.gov/Census/2003Census.pdf.

114

50.   Walker, James Loy. The Regulator Movement: Sectional Controversy in North Carolina, 1765-1771. Graduate thesis. Louisiana State University, 1962. Print.

51.   Ward, H. Trawick, and Davis, Jr., R.P. Stephen. "Time before History: The Archaeology of North Carolina." Chapel Hill: University of North Carolina Press, 1999. Print.

52.   Whittenburg, James Penn. Backwoods Revolutionaries: Social Context and Constitutional Theories of the North Carolina Regulators, 1765-1771. Graduate thesis. University of Georgia, 1974.

CPSIA information can be obtained at www.ICGtesting.com
Printed in the USA
LVOW091429060613

337344LV00001B/27/P